CRYPTIC CLOCKWORK

A Journey of Words Through Loss and Finding Hope

Renley N. Chu

EDITED BY TIFFANY CHU

Printed in the United States of America

Cover design © Richard Ljoenes

ISBN: 978-1-7377727-1-2 (paperback)

ISBN: 978-1-7377727-2-9 (hardcover)

ISBN: 978-1-7377727-5-0 (ebook)

For Roo,
my everything.

"He will wipe every tear from their eyes. There will be no more death or mourning or crying or pain, for the old order of things has passed away."
Revelation 21:4 NIV"

Contents

Author's Preface

This book is a series of poems and prose, revolving around some tough times, and how coping gradually changed my perception of the ordeals.

This project's purpose is just to let out mundane rants and silent opinions that are in no way meant to be harmful, disrespectful, or negative toward anyone. They're a means of coping and getting out unresolved feelings in a healthy manner.

Each part is written individually, and no previous context is needed to enjoy any one part.

If anyone is going through anything and needs someone to talk to, do not hesitate to dm me. I'll try my best to help and listen.

— Renley N. Chu

Author's Acknowledgements

This collection is by no means edited, and hence the poems/prose are as they were written the first time around, between June 2020 and May 2021.

While reading, know these are all amateur writings, done during apprehensive times, with no professional or final intent initially. They are a series of pent-up words that even after writing them down feel distasteful and incomplete. Upon insistence, I have decided to publish for only one person: Arwen.

To Arwen, as you read these, I hope you enjoy them, and can see the value that I do not see in them. They are not the greatest but hold more value because of you.

All that aside, I'm thankful for Bisma, who helped keep it afloat as I was writing, and Marwa, who was eager to edit this half-effort at writing a collection.

— Renley N. Chu

Editor's Dedication

Forever my Kochan, my beloved, my darkling, my 知己, my everything, my soul,

We always said there are no words adequate enough to describe who we are to each other, though we always tried anyway. And I know I will fail, as usual, but I'll still try.

You once sent me a quote that said,

"There's a Japanese phrase that I like: koi no yokan. It doesn't mean love at first sight. It's closer to love at second sight. It's the feeling when you meet someone that you're going to fall in love with them. Maybe you don't love them right away, but it's inevitable that you will." //Nicola Yoon

It seems somehow, we both always knew we were meant to be, though it took us some time to admit that to each other. It seemed that our meeting was a burst of starlight on the black canvas of our lives, a collision of fate, and of souls, and of everything and everything.

Perhaps we didn't know it then, but we needed each other.

And we certainly didn't know it then, but we also saved each other.

There's a strange, inexplicable connection we have, an inexplicable similarity in our experiences, thoughts, and how we view the world. I have marveled more than once at how we were brought together, how I could have spoken understanding and hope into your soul because of what we have shared. How incredibly in sync we always are with each other. It seems impossible, impossible that two people could have a connection like ours, yet so we did.

My darkling, it didn't take long for us to realize what we have is special—so special that neither of us seemed to be able or willing to share much of each other to anyone else; perhaps we feared that giving a name to what we were might break the magic of it.

But slowly we did, and it didn't shatter. We reached across countries and oceans, intertwining our hearts and souls until they became one. Or maybe we were always one, and it just took a bit of time to realize it ourselves. Gradually others began to notice, but still no one truly knows fully how together we are, as two ropes might braid over one another and solidify into one cord of unbreakable steel.

The hours we spent together, day after day, endlessly connected, until we became like air to each other as we helped each other breathe.

Life has been so unkind to us. We both know it wasn't fair. And many times, we've had to convince the other, "Don't let go. Don't let go," until it became our refrain.

"Don't let go. Don't let me go."

"I won't. I won't."

My beloved, we gave each other purpose, a reason to fight for life. Because as long as we knew the other was there, that knowledge was enough to give us something to cling onto amidst all the pain of living. Because as long as the other was there, we knew there was something greater than us to fight for. You held my breath, and I held yours, you once said.

My Kochan, no one will ever know how deeply I love you or how deeply you love me. There is no vocabulary rich enough for what we are. We ourselves were never able to put it into words, and we call ourselves writers. The best we could say was that we are each other's 知己. We are each other's very soul.

You have said no one has seen you the way I see you; no one knows you the way I know you. It became such that even through the limitations of text and distance, we could know what the other was about to say before they said it, sense each other—our moods, our thoughts, things that lay secret and unspoken, the dark corners of our souls that we were afraid of ourselves. We saw it all, knew it all, and we loved each other even more.

My everything, you are the purest, kindest soul I have ever encountered. In spite of all life has put you through, you rise above the dark and give so freely of yourself to others, to me. It is the greatest privilege of my life to know you and for you to call me yours, as you are also mine. From the beginning, I have said you are incredible, so incredible. You rose from brokenness and ashes with your soul intact, and all the horror you have seen and experienced has never darkened your brilliant light.

The world is utterly unworthy of you.

It has never deserved you, but for eighteen years, it held you in it, and you shine, my darkling, you shine so, so brightly. You always will.

You never could see fully what I see in you, but I think you caught a glimpse of it, because you are so secure in my love for you. Some hidden part must have known you are worthy of such love. And you, my beloved, you have, and will always be, worthy. You will always be beautiful, so beautiful to me, in every way a person can be.

You said I was impossible because you couldn't understand how I could see all of you and still stay. You always asked me why I love you, and I could only say that I simply do; there has never been a reason, and there never needed to be one. I love you for yourself: — nothing more and nothing less.

We promised each other we would be together and that you would come home to me, but heaven had other plans, and the hope we clung to for so long will now never come to fruition. And I must try to live on without you, for you. But how am I to live without my soul?

On that last day, when you knew it was ending, through the nightmare of knowing we would soon be parted, still I am grateful, grateful I was there with you until your very last breath, grateful you knew to the end that with me you were safe, that you were loved, grateful to have been with you to the last beat of your heart.

In the last months, as our hope kept delaying, as it ebbed to and fro, we began saying something new. Because by then we knew we would never let go as long as the other was still there. Because we each made life worth living for the other. And it became a phrase that became our new refrain whenever we were losing hope, or when our vision was blurring—over and over we said it to one another, daily, endlessly, and it is what we said to each other again and again, even on that last day. Because this love is ours only, and we are each other's.

"Tell me again what you know is true."

"I am yours and you are mine."

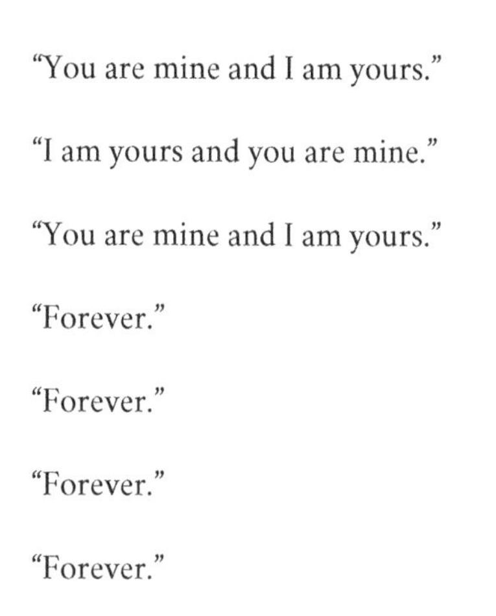

"You are mine and I am yours."

"I am yours and you are mine."

"You are mine and I am yours."

"Forever."

"Forever."

"Forever."

"Forever."

"Forever."

My Kochan, my 知己, I love you so much, so much. And though such words still fall so, so short of what I feel for you, I say again that I love you, and I love you forever.

I miss you so much.

"A love that would change the constellations and the reality of existence," you once wrote of us. And so it has, my Kochan. So it has. For us.

Forever your Roo, your safe place, your home,
your 知己, your fairy, your everything, your soul

INTRODUCTION

All pieces have been copied in their entirety with minor edits, in order to retain as much of the author's original intents and words as possible while improving clarity and flow. Letters are mildly edited to exclude personal information for the sake of privacy.

Pieces are arranged by subject, and somewhat chronologically. This begins with the loss of Renley's parents and continues through his experiences in his abusive adoptive family, the loss of a close friend through suicide, and a toxic, abusive relationship with his ex-boyfriend. They give a glimpse into Ren's internal state as he processed through past and ongoing trauma, his grief, inability to speak, struggles with mental health, and homophobia.

Despite a life marked by tragedy, Ren maintained his purity of heart, compassion, and resilience. He fought—harder than anyone I have ever known—to triumph over impossible circumstances that threatened to quench his beautiful spirit, to live. For someone so physically fragile, he is the bravest and strongest person to have ever crossed my path.

As you read, you will hopefully notice Renley's journey and personal growth, from someone who molded himself to what his abusers needed, to finding his own identity and voice, and from aimless despair to joyful hope as he found his reason to live.

—Tiffany Chu (Arwen)
Editor

About the Author

Born in England as Leonel M. M. Santiago on May 14, 2003, Renley lost both his parents in a fire that permanently damaged his vocal cords and lungs at the age of five in October 2008, leaving him unable to speak. He became Justin Steele at the age of eight when adopted into the Steele family, a place in which he endured unspeakable horrors.

Midway through 2020, Ren began writing intensively, continuing until his death, producing this whirlwind of a collection of his prose and poems, written entirely during that short period. Each piece exudes the rawness and authenticity of his heart, his emotions, his experiences.

At the beginning of 2021, even as his health rapidly deteriorated, we began making plans for Ren to become our family and bring him to the United States. On May 18, 2021, he changed his legal name to Renley Nicolas Chu.

About a week after his eighteenth birthday, Renley succumbed to his poor health and passed away on May 25, 2021, the day he wrote the last piece in this collection (Happiness). It was three days before he would have come home. He called me from the hospital when he knew he was passing, and we stayed on call together for his last hours until the last beat of his heart.

Though we were never to be physically together, our hearts were connected in such a way that transcended distance, even fate. He died knowing he was deeply loved and wanted, that there was finally a place and people to which he belonged. He died happy and at peace.

Renley's last wish to come home was fulfilled on June 1, when his ashes were brought to San Diego and scattered at Los Peñasquitos Canyon.

Despite the suffering he endured throughout his short life, Ren never lost his remarkable purity of heart. He always treated each person as a beautiful, worthy individual, deserving of his attention and care. Regardless of how he was feeling, regardless of his own struggles, he did all in his power to make each person's life better. In the short time he was here, he imprinted himself onto the hearts of countless people, whether they knew him well or not. He is remembered as one of the most compassionate people one would ever have the privilege of coming across. Though he had seen so much more of the evil in humanity than most people will ever encounter in their entire lives, he retained a loving, kind heart, devoid of any lasting bitterness, giving freely to all.

He had no voice to speak with, yet here his words will live on forever and leave his mark upon the world. He had no voice, but through his writing, the world will finally hear him as he deserved to be heard.

I love you so much forever, my Kochan.

Tiffany Chu (Arwen)
Your Roo, always, only

Renley Nicolas Chu
(May 14, 2003-May 25, 2021)
The world was not worthy of you

Part One

The Beginning

An Introduction of Sorts

Personality—As the people who have been talking to me know, my personality is a literal tornado. It can go from a mean piece of shit to a sarcastic battle machine to a huge mess in literal seconds. But it has a calm to it at the very top where the eye of the hurricane is.

A memory—A hue of green-tinted sunlight that filters through the leaves high above—this canopy of comfort where we used to go camp, near a serene lake deep within the camping site. A rickety dock and feet in the water swishing around the cold purity of the lake, with an anxious mother behind, making sure I'm alright.

My parents—A blurry haze of dark brown hair and my brown eyes, soft locks that framed her beautiful face so very perfectly. Slender hands that swiped my grandma's enchiladas from my plate because I hated them. I might be forgetting how you looked, how you sounded, but I've written about you too many times to forget the things you did for me, Mum. Rest in peace.

A fuzzy memory of my dirty blonde nest atop a square head, greenish brown eyes, crinkled eyes. An itchy beard and calloused hands that removed the trainers from my bike on a rainy day because I was a stubborn child. I may not be able to picture you anymore, but I remember the man you were, and I hope to be the same one day.

LEO

Later in the hours after the deed, it's always quiet—no hum of machinery and no static from light bulbs—just this subdued stillness, settled at the very core of your being.

The wind is fast and ominous—so much so that it makes everything seem suspended.

The orange is gone, and the chilly stasis in the air doesn't bother you at all—you're stuck—stuck in the orange, and the warmth, and the undeniable urge to have it swallow you whole.

The irony doesn't cease to taunt you as the delicate sides of your throat feel scorched: this house you've come to truly mold with, now a corpse holding everything and everyone you hold dear. Everyone but you.

But it is you, and you're left with that thought: still young, and still naive, and still so very confused. Because death was never this real before. Death was just a word, a peaceful sleep that Grandma had stumbled upon.

Not this. Not this harsh, burning moment that has torn everything you've known to shreds. The licks of flames are so spectacular, you can feel them alive, as if they live to consume.

The blue and red in the background only make the orange come out as the sky darkens, leaving grey smoke all around. Grey, suffocating smoke that's destroyed the words you would've wanted to say, you would've wanted to tell, to scream.

They're gone, buried with everything else, and you just let whoever has their hand on your shoulder lead you away to crowded rooms and so much noise—noise that you hate with this passion, because none of it is yours, no matter how much you try.

And you stay buried somewhere, deep in the noise out of sight, until this jolly idiot comes in one day. Obnoxious and arrogant, but real. Sincere.

And he takes you along and forces you to meticulously come out of this nonexistent grave you've hidden yourself within. And he seems warm. Not like the fire. But like the summer: —this yellow hollow, and this person your childish mind has been yearning for since they died.

You ignore his parents and turn to him, and he raises you and nurtures you, and it's too much and—and it's too little, and you're again suspended in this balance you've missed since this distant blur.

Because you're forgetting everything but that night and it's still eating you up. How can you forget them?

You fall again in this morbid cycle of writing everything you can, and you read it again and again to make sure you don't forget. Because it's where you come from. You're not this new person; you're still Leo.

And as much as you want to embrace this skin, you don't want to forget what happened. Because you want to be your own person. Your own being. You want to be Leo and you want to hate Leo.

You want to keep Leo alive because you don't want to insult the memory of this boy buried in the noise. He existed. And you want him remembered.

So you write his story. Again and again. And you'll keep writing Leo's story because he might not be you now; no, you've fallen far below him, but you were once Leo. And Leo deserved better.

Because Leo died that night too, but he died a worse death than the others. He wasn't asleep like Grandma. He was this ghost. This ghost that lived within the new you.

And you like that. You like that you're this translucent ghost because it's safe here. And it's far away from that house surrounded by orange, and because you're far away from this chaotic mortal, and it's safe because you can be both: both Leo and this new person you've been shown to embrace.

And you're okay.

For today.

And when you're not, you'll write the story again. And it will make it okay. Because you're not forgetting. Not now. You've written both Leo and this ghost down so many times. Scattering clues of both boys' existence. So you can be at peace.

And you're okay.

And it's all that matters for today.

Stove Knobs

You were playing with the stove knobs.

I probably, maybe, remember that, but it may as well just be something I've created; I don't know. I don't know.

I wish I could remember and forget, or maybe let go but remember, but then comes more from sources I barely know.

You were playing with the stove knobs.

And everyone seems to know that.

Everyone.

If only it was set out clearly—not so blurred. If only I could trust myself to remember it right for once.

Instead, it's a game of eavesdropping and gauging, since no one will tell me more.

You were playing with the stove knobs.

A light bulb. And smoke.

You were playing with the stove knobs.

But then why be so hell bent on just that?

You were playing with the stove knobs.

How do I know I can trust you?

How do I know I can trust me?

You were playing with the stove knobs.

And again, just that.

Except I really want to know what to do with this artificially significant ignition.

You were playing with the stove knobs.

Maybe it's remembering the wrong things: playing with stove knobs and fire, closed casket funerals, and denial.

Only being used in all ways possible, and giving up not once, not twice, sadly not even thrice—so many times that it's futile to keep count.

And how memory is so faulty and unreliable—a façade being built upon every other thing you hear and salvage—for no one deems you good enough to know more.

Like how despite wanting to picture it all, you can barely see flickers of a previous life: blonde and brown hair, crinkled eyes and kind beards.

Even those images are corrupted by doubt and the futility of this useless human mind.

If only there was more to this comedic tragedy—more than irony and inevitable disappointment.

Makes you wonder whether writing them down for your convenience is even worth it anymore.

If clutching so hard is worth the effort and the ache.

Remember Remembering

I remember remembering you, your humor and your nerve; and I remember remembering him, his valor and his curse.

But as time glides through, so peacefully amidst this rocky terrain, I apologize for forgetting how the two of you looked.

I apologize for letting go of who you were, and I apologize immensely for writing down what I thought was.

The jigsaw of broken memories often collapses. Mum, I try to keep the integrity of your tan skin and brown hair, but like all that's good, it fades into wisps of smoke.

I try living on, as a remnant of who you were, but the immense distance is too big a cleft to grip and latch on to.

And while I try holding onto the tiny pictures from the past, I often forget to keep up with him.

I forgot him first, and perhaps it's why addressing him hurts the most. But I've written him down, as truly as possible.

Unlike with you, I can only imagine his crinkled eyes and proud beard.

But I remember remembering the both of you. I truly do.

And that hurts more because had memory been a friend, I would never have let you fade from my book.

I remember remembering though, and it's not what we'd truly wish for, and it hurts more this way. But at least I remember remembering you.

Poetic End

A cold room and warm duvets. The static before sleep, and this lull of peace just dangling afar. Yet in hindsight, it seems to be this long, endless slumber my body longs for, and an eternal rest on damp ground six feet under, where no human can exhaust this tired conscience.

The time is set for everyone, yet I still sometimes wonder if I can gain some feeble control over what happens.

Perhaps pray?

When the time comes, however near or far,

I picture high fires and dancing flames. This poetic end to how it started.

It's not that I want a peaceful gateway, nor a serene end.

I need this abrupt spread of pain and this agony. I want to know how they felt, only slower and more excruciating.

I want to bask in the fact that I look just like they did. Not even a casket for closure.

I want to dissolve into ashes and be set off into roaring oceans, complementing my existence and end.

Burning Rage

Far beyond, a land unfathomable, with nothing but night skies and eternal sleep,

maybe I could burn away there—this hollow piece of flesh, one last burden upon these lands.

A cathartic show to those who seek, a burning rage burrowed within,

just maybe you'll hear the screams. Just maybe. As a putrid cage comes, letting out a hidden voice finally seems besieged.

And maybe as the flesh melts away and the bones are made to dust, when not a single living cell can fathom to emerge,

this shallow pool of once-existing life can finally feel the breeze, this cool air that just before, I couldn't seem to feel.

The end will not matter. Not really, you see. It will be a welcomed event, eagerly awaited, right after my purpose is fulfilled.

MERRY CHRISTMAS

December 25, 2020

Dearest Parents,

12 *years*. 1 *mont**h***. 25 *days*.

9 ***h**ours*. 20 *minutes*.

23 *minutes **ha**h**a***.

23 *minutes*.

24 *mins*.

31 *minutes*.

There's this insurmountable feeling always there—this lingering, taunting feeling, presence, void. Something. Maybe it's just a what if? Or just this, what was. Or maybe it's just me justifying something that is not really there, because you existed, and then you didn't, and I was too young. Too young. Too young.

I mean, twelve years ago. Way too young. Maybe I shouldn't remember what I have salvaged in these glass jars. I like to shake them every so often and awaken what's inside.

There's a grey jar, and a green jar, and a brown one, and also this pink one. I think, Mum, you'd like the red one. And Dad would laugh and cherish the blue one.

I personally really like shaking the purple one. It likes to play with me a bit by not working sometimes. Have to shake it real hard. Turn off all the lights and all the sounds and sit under the blanket and try really hard.

It has you, Mum, and later Dad. And I'm wearing skates. The smallest skates. And I'm on the carpet. But I'm still wearing knee and elbow pads, and I have a helmet on. And my balance isn't as good as Juan's. And I'm most likely still going to fall, but I'm laughing in breathy, high-pitched, weird intervals.

And it's nice because the light is warm and orange. And Dad is telling me how to position my feet. And Mum, you are too scared and just want me to take them off and sit on the couch instead.

48 *minutes.*

I like to play with the purple jar quite often. Sometimes I think of opening and spilling its contents though. Sometimes I feel like the purple jar doesn't exist and I've just made it up.

Sometimes, sometimes I wish I could physically be there and smell the air and feel the skates on my feet. Sometimes I wish I could sit on the couch and resume Pinocchio so we could finish it. 'Cause I haven't watched the whole film, ever. And now I really, really want to, and yet don't want to.

51 *minutes.*

51.

Right now though, right now I really just want to shake the jar and see it again. All of them. The orange, the blue, the pink and green and brown and red.

But I can't. I can't. I want to. But I can't.

54 *minutes.*

I hope wherever in the summit you are, you can't see what goes on below. And I hope wherever in the summit you are, you never read this. And I hope however it is up there, it's pretty and orange and purple and green and pink and blue.

56 *minutes.*

I hope we never cross paths again. I hope that somewhere, if the family up there exists, I hope you have a Leo. And that he's whatever I couldn't be to you. I hope he's everything you dreamed him to be. I hope he's everything I want to be to you.

Merry Christmas.
With lots of love,
Leo.

Dancing Beneath Rainfall

January 23, 2021

"It's dark, and brown, with an orange gleam; warm, not burning. A redemption towards then."

There's a brown shelf, and it has all the files you need for work. It's downstairs, and although I know that room is for work, I often just go and sit there. I can't address you; it feels like I shouldn't, but you let me sit in the big chair that swallowed me. You'd tell me not to touch Mum's things because they're important and she'll get in trouble if they get lost, and then you'd go back to work.

You have lots of books and tell me about how you teach your students about snow being endings, and mountains being constants, and about elephants having a good memory, and about plays by Arthur Miller and Shakespeare that I don't seem to remember now.

The room is hazy with fog, and dark, but it's brown with a warm, nice orange illuminating its edges. The bookshelf is filled with jars, and I've arranged them from the foggiest jars first to the colorful ones at the end. The colors swirl around inside the jars with the white fog of unsure, forgotten moments, mixed with certain ones looking like marble.

"The night was free, and it wasn't terrifying. It wasn't terrifying."

I like the green one; it's green because I remember your hoodie being green. I remember wearing the same hoodie, even as young as I was, with a torchlight, snuggling into a ball and pretending to be a gnome after playing in the rain.

You used to love January, and rain, and at night when I'd be up trying to open my window because I wanted to feel the rain, I remember you waking up and laughing at my wet sleeves.

Instead of getting mad, I remember you telling me to quietly follow, and I remember spending a few moments outside with you in the rain.

You told me they were tired, held my hand, and looked at the clouds.

"They're just tired of crying; do you know why?"

I remember saying it's because they didn't want to hide the moon. And you chuckled and said I'd grow up to be a great writer. Because even then, I remember saying my book would be on your shelf one day.

You said they're tired—tired because they were created. And everything is eventually worn out and tired; it's the only way their story can be read. Our thoughts had danced under the rain and soaked each other's presence, and we had gone back to bed fulfilled.

Your dad tells me you hate birthdays; he tells me you hated them because everyone has swerved off-track from what the actual purpose is. Instead of being grateful for being given the chance to prove ourselves to Him, we celebrate the years that we've lived, marking them as milestones, forgetting we all go. We all go one day, eventually.

Happy birthday. Happy birthday to you.

Again, Before I Forget

Stringing in incoherence, and mustering just enough breath, he spoke softly, gently, his voice rough, but otherwise soft.

"Please."

His finger moved around the pool of mesmerizing water, reflecting off a metallic color. As if a pool of mercury, tinted blue, flowed beside the barren brown dirt.

"Just this once."

He continued, the finger turning in circles. "Show me."

His voice echoed from the surroundings, gentle and calm. His finger stopped twirling in the water. Taking it out, he watched the metallic liquid tainting the tip of his index. Drops of the surprising water, like liquid falling back into the flowing stream.

"Show them to me. Show them to me, please."

The only sounds: the running and magical liquid flowing toward the ocean to be lost, and the voice echoing and echoing and echoing.

For a second, the boy's heart beat a bit faster, building in momentum, eyes diminishing as he stared at the stream sadly. And right after, he turned to see where he now lay, in a room. A little toy room. He smiled, standing up, still tired, still weary.

As if he was an intruder in this perfect, beautiful haven.

He walked slowly, drinking in the house's little details: the walls, not black with angry, scorched marks, but painted a pretty brown. The stairs are wooden, and at the bottom, carpeted.

He stepped down each stair and explored every perfect corner of the house.

And he went around and around, drinking it all in until he found them, all seated perfectly, himself included: his parents, brother, and grandfather.

And afterwards he walked back to the room and lay on his stomach as he had before, blinking once, twice, keeping in the details, as he finally found himself back beside the water.

Index finger going back into the stream, a trailing scar from the finger to his elbow apparent.

With breathing a chore, and existence bringing this prickling feeling, making him claw things out of himself that he didn't want yet to come out.

Mustering up another bout of comprehension and stringing again, "Please. Again, and again, and again until I'm gone."

Voice still gentle but heard. "Again, and again. And again."

Sounds of only the running metallic, watery liquid. And echoes.

"Show them to me. Before it disappears again. Show them to me."

"Again and again and again and again."

In Time's Canister

May 12, 2021

Time.

It binds you, holds you within invisible rails, and passes by, drop by drop, filling the canister you're sitting still in.

As my canisters fill, I forget you a little more every day. You're a little blunter every day, submerged in the milky white of time's fault. Or my fault.

And every time I'm conscious of it, it seems as though it has passed by fast, despite the slow trickle of moment after moment that all seem to hold some problem or other.

I chose green for him because at that moment, he was just mine, and as such I chose blue for you because in blue, you were all mine.

This year it's a little whiter, unclear. I read all of what I wrote of blue the previous years on this day, and they seem foreign even as I try to remember they're mine.

I wonder if this is time neglecting memory, or whether it's just me abandoning things because I no longer hold any capacity for anything.

It rained today, and I was reminded of open windows and wet sleeves, your brown stool that helped me get to the droplets outside.

I think I remember the stool more clearly than I remember you, but maybe that's because inanimate objects are still and permanent like that.

We humans are meant to fade away to become the version others need, or don't need. Some of them like to torment you even when you're gone.

Things are on a path to the better though. I'm going home soon, and maybe then, I can make sure to crystalize each jar before they turn white. Maybe I can write down their clarity in safety before time turns them turns them white.

*Happy birthday to **you**.*

Part Two

Woeful Trajectory

Night

The wind is crisp, the ground wet, and the sound of droplet after droplet steady.

The night is dark and cloudy, and the shadows seem to get larger and morph into something more life-like, into things that linger even after the night is gone.

There's a bark, and maybe sometimes a car that passes by, and either way your heart thumps louder, and you huddle into yourself, out of sight.

The wet grass tickles, and the drops are now warm, because even the cold can do only so much for this long.

The corner near the bush seems ideal, smaller, but you think it'll be warm; you just have to wait until your skin's cold enough for the temperature to become a norm.

Just have to wait until the sun can peek through, and the birds fly by, and for the foggy stasis to pass by.

Maybe you'll even doze off for a while; that's not good though, because she says she looks forward to the day you don't wake up from these nights.

You can hear this whistling presence of the everlasting nothing, and how inevitably it can only seem like the haunting song from something wrong.

Like how the night comes with this tall presence, with a dark thick coat, and tears, and a crooked nose, with no hope and no stop.

The black, endless sky that even on highways seems suffocating, and has your breath shortening, and limbs quivering for no reason other than this endlessness.

As if maybe one day, the sun might never come up. Maybe the door would never open. Maybe your skin will frost over and stop your heart from struggling so hard.

TEARS

"Why did you cry?"
'hm?'

"That night, when we cancelled plans?"

Didn't know you'd seen me.

'because sometimes tears aren't bad'.

A walk.

We used to walk a lot. So there are walks and there are ***those*** walks.

But for now, ***a*** walk.

The sun had set long ago; in fact, people were snug under the covers, away from the world of the 'awake' hours beforehand.

Yet here we were, clad in winter coats and no gloves or hat. You only hated the cold because of its apparent futility.

And because we knew we'd feel too warm, as slowly we became accustomed to it anyhow.

I had started this small "tradition" of ours.

And I also had a knack of reminding you why.

'She never got tired, even when I'd be wheezing for breath.'

And you'd tint red, not in cold, but in anger. As if she wasn't a friend, but a lover.

Though we both know your insecurity came from the fact that she was more to me than you could ever be, lover or not.

And that spoke volumes on your awareness as well as ours.

But also because I would never give that spot to anyone else.

•———— · ☾ ☽ · ————•

Sometimes tears aren't bad.

Doesn't make them any less tragic though.

Sometimes we can't be trusted with intent.

Doesn't make us any less trustworthy though.

•———— · ☾ ☽ · ————•

Ninth October.

"I don't think I can stay; Mum needs me to help her for tomorrow night. Need to take her shopping."

'Okay.'

Relief. Maybe too much. And tears.

"Okay, see you, stay safe, yeah? Will be with you the day after tomorrow like I promised."

'It's okay. Don't die.'

A chuckle. A much more aware chuckle then I had estimated.

"Why did you cry?"

'hm?'

"That night, when we cancelled plans?"

Didn't know you'd seen me.

'because sometimes tears arent't bad'.

She would have jumped into that too-high bricked separator protecting the grass and laughed like a proud madwoman.

"You really don't possess a brain, do you?"

'Nope.'

"I always knew you were irredeemable."

She'd be proud. And angry. But proud.

"It's the tears that come from more than sadness, more than anger—the tears that leave you numbed blissfully by the end; those are the tears I'll cry when you've finished your goddamned homework."

- Elke

"I'd cry those tears at your deathbed, or mine. I'd cry those tears not out of mirth or grief—but out of the crushing and suffocatingly typical existence of everything but us."

- Elke

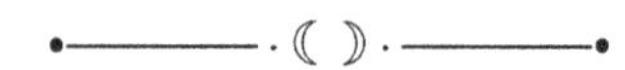

So instead of picking up the pieces of herself and piecing them together, she gave those pieces away to those she claimed—or rather, deluded herself into thinking—needed them more.

And slowly as each piece was given away, and each time she fell deeper, she became one with the earth, one with the ground, one with the universe.

More content than anyone I had ever seen plunging to death.

"It was everyone but you," she said.

Doesn't that make it no one but me?

She helped me more than I could ever help her, showed me more than I could ever show anyone. She impacted so much, so much. She didn't even stay long enough for me to tell her that. She didn't stay long enough to know.

But that's the thing: some people who want to leave don't stay long enough to have people know something is wrong.

She died happy. I've never seen anyone die so happy.

Are You Happy?

The stars had shone brightly that one night, a rare sight in the city, but I could feel this dread churning at the pit of my stomach.

We'd broken apart ages ago, but it seems only now that that had been unveiled. Perhaps it was a denial on both our parts that made us latch on more.

"I'm done."

And you weren't, but I guess it was another show of vigor, a scare tactic that I'd been waiting on desperately.

And you left, and for the first two hours of the night, everything remained calm, the moonlight brighter, and the stars twinkling above.

Despite the wrong that I could make out hidden beneath the freedom.

This small rebellious streak afterwards had resulted in aggravated grownups and a satisfying stay in my room downstairs, where a swift decision of something so mundane introduced me to a whole library of good influences.

And things were still great; everything was better than ever, but the previous sense of doom had started tingling, forcibly coming to the top, demanding attention.

And I buried it, continuing this growing agenda of writing and posting and writing and posting.

The time came when squashing it all down became detrimental in ways I hadn't thought of before.

All that was left was stillness and routine that left more time to think and more time to dwell until I wanted out.

Like a veil had replaced the ignorance and now, even that small commodity was shedding, slowly and more intensely.

I wanted to go back to no posts, and you, and no people I could trust—a responsibility that now felt heavy in a way.

For one way or another, I was meant to disappoint, what with a crippled conscience and the need for a crutch to see life with.

Now the stars are back to dim lights—one or two if you look closely—and cold nights that have me lying in bed more often than doing anything unless 1it's work.

The feeling of doom and dread and sheer fear is still here, like an aching part of me rebelling and trying its best to tear me down.

But I don't want to leave what I have now, nor let go of what had previously taken place.

I want to remain at a safe distance from enjoying what each has to offer, while I give all I can from afar.

Because giving is always less heavy than receiving, and way lighter than the burden of troubles that shouldn't be deployed for anyone to bear.

I'm fine and not fine: this acatalepsy in between the two that keeps me okay, helps me stay and not stay at the same time.

Ordinary Moments

Times weren't always stormy with you around; there were snippets of this friend that I had once come to cherish more than anyone else in just a few weeks' time.

Snippets of walks in the cold, leaving behind barren houses and crowded halls. Cooking, and how you were so remarkably awful at it.

I remember times where it used to be brighter, and it felt light spending all the ordinary moments I could muster with you, as if what was to come around afterwards couldn't even summon the energy to ruin them.

Snippets of a person, maybe a façade of one, or maybe just who you once were, trying to help a cause that from almost every direction seemed hopeless.

You need to know: you helped. You helped. Maybe hopeless in the end, but it was a less unsavory existence just because of your presence. But only in those moments.

And to be honest, I didn't regret crossing a boundary in making you more than my friend. But it's been made so, that calling you more than a friend makes my body recoil and my hands shake.

But I knew this person once that seemed quite forward, quite sincere. I felt worthy of him, if only for a second.

And I prided myself in choosing right for once, however long it had been. Because it seemed as though I knew you.

You were always thinking ahead of time to get me ordinary things, and show me kindness, and provide a firm hold when I almost always wanted to slip.

Funny how long you prolonged that, for no reason than to fulfill your own need.

And ordinary moments stretched further away from each other with time, and the person I knew started to rot from the outside to his very core.

I'm not mourning you (or maybe I am), but I'm mourning the you I lost within barely two months of our encounter. I'm mourning the light and warm ordinariness that chased away and reprimanded my demons.

I'm mourning the simple acts of homework, and cooking, and movies, and talking, and walking.

I'm mourning the person I knew, or that I thought I knew. And I'd be lying if I say I don't miss who you became either; I find myself thinking of the new person you embodied as a necessity of sorts.

But the you I knew way before: simple, ordinary and light—I miss him the most, and I saw him, a couple of times, merged into who I suppose you really were.

And that might've tainted it, but it doesn't make it hurt any less; if anything, it hurts more. And the death of who you are wasn't as apparent before, but now it seems to be a constant thought.

As if who you were is haunting me into going back, if only to bring back to life who you are.

Irrevocable Cloning

In the distance, not too far, just there in a corner, where communication seems futile and words incoherent, a seldom-seen figure, eyes alight, might be gazing right your way.

The look of a manic sociopath makes you still—because you know this seldom-seen figure—and you don't. This frustrating battle where you determine whether the man in the corner is the one you know, or the cold man that comes out at times.

You play this game every day, at times wondering if you're the same breed—this, this docile man doomed to the world and beyond, only to bloom into the very man you're wary of.

In the end it doesn't matter because you're still here, and the guy in the corner doesn't stray; you forget this waltz, and at the end you have no other choice but to dip.

And you relax, smile, and turn, popping two pills into the orange drink in your hand so discreetly that even you don't notice. The accuracy scares you and eases you.

You don't care if this irrevocable man will be a monster today.

It's way too blurred.

Too incoherent to keep the man and monster apart.

Afterwards, when the drink is finished and he lays on the couch, that gleam in his eyes belongs to you as you stare around at each one of the young students from the corner.

And when someone stills at your gaze, you lower yours and move out, disturbed and horrified at the irreversible conversion from who you were to who he is.

Condemned Us Both

It started subtle—slow and easy.

We found each other when we needed us the most, and we built ourselves up to start the long walk of life's propagating onslaught.

Superimposing on each other's lives and building on each other's foundation until it became a fight of who looked the best.

I never thought of it that way, but I'd be lying if I said I didn't want to be better.

It worked like a well-oiled machine, the output at first brilliantly addictive.

Except his better was on the outside, and mine on the inside.

And soon, with each passing day, this difference started chipping away, rusting the screws and knobs.

It became a detriment. Instead of sticking closer like magnets attracting to opposite poles, we started a feud.

He won because I let him. And we continued this way. I let him win for however many rounds the future held. Only because winning wouldn't be beneficial for me in the end.

"Justin," he'd say some days, "why me?"

And I'd be speechless, because inside while I developed, I knew he was detrimental. It was inevitable he'd destroy what he'd helped build.

It's what all creators do, isn't it? Create until they finish, and then start on a new project, the last one obviously not as refined as the more recent ones.

I'd have no choice though, in his arms on a bed, watching the same old movies again and again; I'd turn to face him, and amidst all the crudeness would be tears—tears I'd wipe away and flash a small smile reserved for him.

'Because I love you.'

I'd lie. Because in the end I didn't—couldn't—share my nothings—just embrace his everythings. Another developmental detriment: I couldn't not accept the small bouts of love I could receive.

Instead, I learned to be nice to everyone, despite differences, despite any foundation between us. I'd be there to offer myself indiscriminately, and everyone could take.

Only because I wasn't equipped to refuse him in the start (or anyone, for that matter), still hoping my cruelty would change. And as I remained unsure for however many more weeks, soon refusal wasn't on the menu.

For it was replaced with fear; I wouldn't dare to leave when consequences hung there, dangling near me just a few paces away. It became another reason to fall deeper yet cling stronger to this—whatever we had.

And afterwards, when all his warnings became just another day in life, and I'd be in bed too spent to get up, he'd be on the other side, on that brown loveseat we'd smash to pieces in the future. He'd say, "Justin." And I'd hold my breath, burrowing deeper into my duvet, when he asked, "Why me?"

And I'd ask myself the same thing, only more frequently, but I couldn't tell him it was because of fear, or my lack of awareness of us and what we were.

So I'd turn away, flashing a hurried, 'because I love you,' before vanishing into my head again.

One time he got up, walking to the bed and sitting next to me, his fingers softly playing with my hair despite the initial flinch.

"I love you too," he said. "I don't deserve you, but I love you too."

And how could I possibly have left him afterwards? How could I possibly have told him I never loved him, that I wanted out? I couldn't.

I condemned the both of us.

I tried fixing the little jagged pieces that stuck out from under his smooth flawless façade, helping him build himself up by tearing pieces of myself and adjusting them on him.

He wore them better anyway.

And soon when I couldn't give more, and things began thinning out, he began demanding the dignity I had left, that little bit of worth

I'd kept for myself. The human things we'd all been born with the privilege of.

And I couldn't not give.

Couldn't refuse. Because I'd condemned us. It was only fair I followed through.

Because it'd be worse for me either way, and accepting was easier than confrontation. Confrontation would lead to it being my fault; besides, I hadn't refused before. It *was* my fault.

And although I gave everything, I wish he'd taken my other limitations too: the doubt and indecisiveness, the nightmares and anxiety.

Because I hadn't loved him; I don't think I've loved anyone that way, but I'd given enough for it to be nothing else. Not in others' eyes.

And so, weeks afterwards, on the floor, I found myself staring out the window; his voice startled me badly, and my heart thumped hard—no tears, but goosebumps racing across my skin, and my breathing coming in small gasps, and he said, "Justin." And I stared at his feet, having not looked into his eyes for months. "Why me?"

And I leaned against his legs, stared out the window, no energy to come up with a response.

Despite the itch at the contact, or the discomfort and fear, I couldn't move away, because there was so much more to endure if I stepped out of bounds.

"I love you too," he said.

And I closed my eyes and tried to steady my heartbeat.

Days later, he brought two others; his excuse: "To keep things exciting." And I wanted to refuse. To run.

But I didn't have the energy. October's cold weather had me paralyzed and things happened. And he left with dirty, green notes in his hand that he shoved in his pocket before I could catch sight. Too late.

But there was not much I could do.

He continued, and after the initial October, I learned to numb myself to it. Numb myself to most of it.

Until he left, and the next October, when he isn't here, I'm left writing just this, with only the remnants coming out with so much more intensity now than they ever did in the past.

And I'd just lay there in a new bed, wallowing and fencing myself from this turmoil that's so much more intense today than it ever was when he was around.

Burning Cycle

It bothers me. Not going to lie: it really bothers me now.

How I still want it, despite hating it, how I still wish someone would be there to keep me in line—enough to not spill and hurt the better people.

All the details of this bigger cage are coming into focus, and I can't escape the onslaught that's toppling out.

And yet I don't want to spill, because it's likely not anyone's concern or burden, just a deranged mind still coping, and a conscience still guilty.

Guilty of the marred skin and vile feeling of limbs that don't seem to feel like mine, guilty of how every single thing feels deserved because there was always a reason ingrained behind each welt and each scar.

But I'm tired of too-hot showers that switch to freezing water, and tired of running nails across dirty skin hard enough to bleed.

Tired of keeping it in and spilling it out.

Guilty of not being able to wallow in what I feel deserving of.

One day I might look back and sympathize, but I don't want to confront that either. And I'm stuck in this vortex where life seems stuck in the past while everyone moves on.

As if I missed a train everyone forgot to inform me I was supposed to board.

Still stuck in this ignorance I can't grace myself enough to escape.

Because I don't want to. I don't want to—but not following through seems a detriment to those around me.

If only, once, so long ago, I hadn't played with the stove knobs.

Let's Dance, Shall We?

I remember the wooden flooring to your grey bedroom; you said minimalism was key behind it. You said you were proud of it, having designed it yourself.

I never said so, but I thought the wood was far too cold, and the walls far too sad; I never said this, but the curtains were way too dark, and the whole atmosphere felt much more suffocating than minimalistic.

In a way, it matched who you were, and so I couldn't really complain. Both of you seemed, from a distance, accommodating. Maybe if we had rarely spent time together, then even something to look forward to once in a blue moon.

Human beings aren't built that way though, no, we like to devour what appeases us. And that's what we did; we devoured each other.

So let's dance, shall we?

Because that's all it was. A dance.

Your words, and me on a pedestal.
The scapegoat to a perpetrator.
Your song, and your strings.
I just followed along.

It took more than the initial fire to get me to dance to your song, but that's fine; I eventually got used to the calculated steps and the fast-paced tune.

You were right though; the room was designed perfectly to your needs. And our needs.

Or maybe those were your needs too.

The belt in your closet, or the extra sheets below the bed. The lock on the doors, and the location far from the house's hub.

Perfect.

Perhaps.

Maybe it was more than the room itself though, like the absent inhabitants and clueless siblings.

In the end, I was just as accommodating as well, letting you do all you pleased, with little, voiceless resistances and distant foreign struggles.

So let's dance, shall we?
Me on your fingertips,
and you twirling me around and around,
this dizzy dip in the very end
where not even you had the decency to catch me.

But I'd be wrong in some ways, for you weren't just a gloomy room that mimicked your freezing grip.

No, you were also a fire: a fire that held me in moments that caught me by surprise.

Kind words and soft touches balancing out the welts and bruises.

Like how you liked it when we'd lay after school on your bed, planning how we'd complete homework. Me on top and your hands in my hair.

Like how you'd get me Coke before class every day, knowing that's the first stop I'd make, the soda cold as I liked it; you'd obviously made an effort to get it without me knowing.

Like how every time the teacher would sigh and tell us we were free to go, you'd already be beside me to grab my bag and talk about the new song you thought I'd absolutely love.

So let's dance, shall we?
With the beat a high and a low,
fast and harsh,
mellowed by the soft and calm,
like the static pause to catch my breath,
maybe just to prepare me for what comes next.

It was confusing, and in a way frustrating; I needed you; I didn't want you. And you needed me; you didn't want me.

We were never in love, just emotionally codependent for the things we both yearned for.

You groomed me to your needs, and I latched onto you for the kind, subtle formalities you were the only one willing to give me.

In the end though, you slowly broke me. Like someone else a while ago had, and like something else a bit earlier than that had.

I didn't care to notice because I was busy justifying it all until the truth muddled together and reformed into the lies.

You were careful. Too careful.

So let's dance, shall we?
Just one more time?
Just so I can make sure.
Make sure that letting go is worth it,
Worth the vulnerable wounds that lay on the other side.

Whether it was me or you, we'll never know, for you could always voice yourself over my written pleas; my voiceless words always went unheard.

Let's dance for one last time; you sing the words and I'll twirl to your whim—this perfect cruelty of nothing but validity; just this time, like all times, I'll try to stray from your song, but your strong words will still keep me encased as my efforts go unheard. And when I topple down, too spent to continue, you'll crouch down, still singing, closing my eyelids and sealing the end once and for all.

What Am I to You

"You know I didn't mean it, right?" The words were cautious, as if the connotation of revealing the awareness of his actions wasn't previously hidden.

"It was all, just, impulse. I don't know how it happens. I don't know how any of it happens," he continued, voice tinged with an urgency.

Happens.

Like he already intended to do it again. "Happens," like in the present, and hence, like in the future to come.

I hadn't touched the topic. I never did. Always was too much of a coward to point it out after the first few times.

It was he who had brought it up (he always, for some bizarre reason, brought it up). The sun had drowned in the sky a few hours ago, leaving us the universe in its natural form.

'it's okay,' I texted.

"No, it's not. Look at you! I did that!" His voice was unhinged in a semi-conscious sort of way; this Alan scared me less than hinged Alan though.

But then maybe unhinged Alan was hinged Alan, and vice versa.

It was the first time in ages he'd even acknowledged his actions, and I couldn't muster the ability to differentiate whether this was yet another ploy or not.

He stepped over the countless miscellaneous clothes scattered around the floor to reach over, sitting on the edge of the bed and extending his hand to touch my face.

My eyes went to his hand reflexively, and I tensed way too noticeably.

"Shit."

His hand stopped, moved back, but decided to settle near my face instead, eyes on a bruise near my cheekbone.

I remember it was the cheekbone because it wasn't from his hand that the bruise had come, but rather a clumsy accident on my part. A rare occurrence, mind you.

I never knew what to do with myself when this part of him showed; I didn't know what my face should have shown and shouldn't have shown, what would change this slightly self-aware Alan back into the person I feared.

So the only thing that came to mind was remaining clueless.

'there's nothing wrong,' I texted.

"But Jay, there is. There is." Why he'd say it like that, and only in those specific times, was a mystery I didn't care to sort out. "There's so much wrong, Justin."

It always frustrated me. I'd wait for him to change back desperately.

'maybe, but we'll figure it out, okay? Don't worry.' I wasn't sure if he read it all, especially since I could never be sure if anyone bothered to read anything I contributed.

Reading disrupts the flow of conversations anyhow; I couldn't blame anyone.

He sighed, shaking his head. "I wish I was to you what you are to me."

'what am I to you?'

His eyes lingered on the screen a long time, as if formulating a response.

He cleared his throat, licking his lips before looking over. My eyes were glued to my question on the screen, and I remained still, even as his hand moved to my hair and gently combed his fingers through them.

"Words don't exist. Not when it comes to people's worth."

'yes, but we use them anyway. What am I to you?'

And if he hadn't last time, he did ignore it this time. I would have rolled my eyes if I wasn't so attuned to this typical nature of his.

People only like to acknowledge what suits them. I do this. You do this. He did this.

We can't be blamed for who we are.

Self-aware Alan lasted two days back then. Two days where I persistently asked who I was to him.

"I love you. That's what you are to me," he said one afternoon right after school.

'and I don't?'

We were walking home; the sun was out for the first time in a while, which did nothing to chase the cold away.

"You." He paused. "You don't know what love is."

'not knowing love makes you incapable of it?'

"No. It makes you insufficient."

Oh.

I Almost Said Goodbye

"

For the first few days, I wanted you back.
The days after that, I was too distracted.
The days after those, I was just there.

"

Now? Now I'm back to those first few days despite a month or two's cleft. Maybe not because of any want, but need.

Because it might bring me back to defense mode, or back to normal, whatever normal is. Because the danger and fear and whatnot might, just might, make me coherent and unaware.

Because being incoherent and way too aware isn't for me. It is, however necessary, still a different sort of terror: where days just go by. And I don't seem to know what happened and what didn't, what I actually interacted with and what I didn't interact with, who said something and was real, and who said something but wasn't real and didn't even happen.

Last night, last night I thought I'd talked with you, not for ten or so minutes, but for hours. I thought, I thought we'd had a full conversation and you missed me, and we were going to go eat seafood once I got out.

I thought you said you hated home these days, and that you wanted me to move back with Judith.

I thought you said you failed math and don't want to face January.

I thought, I thought I said I missed you too, and that it's boring and cold here.

I thought I was not here, but back there, where you lived next door and we could meet so very frequently.

I thought I told you I regret things, and I thought you apologized but said you wouldn't have it any other way.

I thought I said no, and yes, and you were just as confused.

I thought. I thought.

I thought you were back to someone you were in the very, very start.

I think. I think I'm just too tired to even hold on anymore no matter how much I'm deceiving myself.

I think. I think I'd rather stop instead of waiting for something on the other side.

Numb

Part One

Some wisps of me, the wisps that like to drift away and dredge back up to make me feel guilty, those wisps really, really wanted it.

However improbable it may seem, and however undignified it is, I think like the moon, this has its phases.

There are days, however scarce, where I'm pretty sure that what you did wasn't only unacceptable but wasn't my fault either.

And then, slowly, like some crude parasite, a doubt starts to fester and feed, only to grow and reach its peak.

Like tonight.

Where I have justified and accepted that what you did was okay; I deserved it for doing all I did.

I deserved it because you didn't, and because regardless of all the jibes and jags we faced along the path, I still took it. I took it all.

"It makes you insufficient."

Perhaps, yes. I couldn't satisfy, and while I was insufficient, you were insatiable in your pursuit to fill yourself up.

We knew each other in forms no one else did, and surprisingly you understood me, in the oddest and most subconscious of things.

The wolf in sheep's clothing might be too elaborate, but I can picture you smiling a little too widely and looking a little too closely.

I can see you and I can tell that while you were a mold of sorts—hollow and empty—I was like clay.

Easily moldable to your needs, however undesirable the notion seemed, but better something than nothing, right?

No, I didn't love you, but I miss you.

I probably didn't want you, but I needed you.

I tried to. I always did.

Tried to change to sync with your needs.

It felt okay, because previously I was still numbed too, because I'd just spent days somewhere isolated, only for you to meet me on the other side.

I couldn't let down another friend. I couldn't bear losing another friend. And back then you were a friend.

I needed to match your pace and your steps, only a little bit behind yours, because that's the way you liked it.

I needed to get used to things, and I almost did—you made sure—and I tried, really, really tried to accept and endure all those things you told me to do.

It wasn't as bad as I'm making it out to be, yet everyone would say otherwise; it doesn't feel like you were as extreme as either I, or they, have made you to be.

You were a good friend, an extreme lover, perhaps even a place to forget with fear; I don't like forgetting, but you made me momentarily forget.

And I think that wasn't so bad.

Part Two

That specific morning was a holiday, because we were back at your place, and it was really late at night.

No one else was home and as much as that meant free reign, the ordeal did not in any way seem appeasing.

Not appeasing didn't mean not deserving though; importance and preference are different, I suppose.

It was dark, a little unnecessarily so, but just for me.

I tried peeking from below the cloth for some vague stream of light, but you made sure I couldn't.

I hadn't agreed. Previously, however reluctantly and however questionably, I would, in one form or another, agree.

This time I hadn't. I hadn't.

And while yes, this was a consequence—I'm sure a fair consequence—I didn't want to see it unfold.

But then if all perpetrators started choosing the consequences, then it wouldn't be fair, would it?

It was dark and I couldn't see, and there were more than one pair of hands.

It was dark, and I couldn't move, and there were at least 3 pairs. And maybe if I hadn't been so subdued, I'd have made out their breathing.

THE LIST

The fault with you is, the things you want to forget remain at the forefront of your sight. No provision for anything but the impending storm.

As if it's this cycle, and you want to get out, but you know it's bound to happen, so why forget?

The daily visits, the list. We do not forget the list, now do we? No, you just have to bring it up, for it decides what is to happen next in the story.

Whether it's going to be a series of squashing down the urge to tense (for it hurts worse when you do) or stopping your own limbs from making it worse.

Or it's just a subdued night with a voice lulling you to sleep, one way or the other; it's obvious you can't fathom doing it alone.

Calm Before the Storm

It was because of the moonlight,
how its rays infiltrated the barren rooms so effortlessly.
It was because of the rain
and the beauty it brought as droplets made a beeline down toward the windowsill,
and because of you,
your voice lulling me to an effortless and deep sleep.
It was because everything conceivable was so irrevocably corruptible.
It was because of all this that everything still seemed in stasis,
like that night so long ago and the nights to come didn't exist.
And oh, how I wanted to word it out,
word out how utterly grateful these times felt
but I was bound to remain silent and enjoy the stop in time
for it is well known
it's always calm before the storm.

Confused Betrayal

Perhaps it was the silence of the words I could never speak, this deafening hug you needed to squash yourself out of.

Or was it the marks that seem to now permanently paint my skin: the crisscrossed evidence of a game still unfulfilled?

I wonder if it was just the violence that finally got to you, this odd revelation that before was veiled behind a begrudged past?

Sometimes I wonder if we were already treading on unbidden time, your hunger consuming the starvation I didn't know I felt.

The thing is, I can only assume, and that makes it worse.

It allows this reverie of thought, a confusing betrayal, to swirl around like clockwork.

An embrace of reality to bring me down from this nonexistent high I had settled atop.

And it makes me wonder, was it me or you at the end that made you move on; was it me or you that had you questioning? I wonder if you see your own confusing betrayal.

One with barely any words, and flashes of scars. One where the guilt of this nonexistent skin eats you up.

UNFULFILLED TREASON

Immersed in the shadows that pool around this small place, I can sense the turmoil this darkness has set up for me. The turmoil I'm responsible for creating.

The rails are more defined, and I can make out the intricate twists and turns these crude metal binds take—rather enthralling, if not beautiful. Intriguing, if not addictive. Frustrating, if not crushing.

It makes me want to vanish, just so I can deal with this—deal with this without time's handles coming down and demanding other necessary things I've been trying to accomplish.

It's more the fact that I couldn't manage what you thought I could. I wasn't what you wanted, and there's probably no one out there fitting the criteria.

No one with the patience or passion to put up with your wants, and it makes me want to create it for you, except embodying that wasn't the best. I tried, but I'm glad I couldn't be that person.

Glad that however long I tried, I was able to detach at the wrong, but still fulfilling, time.

Now, as I hear the tell-tales of what is going around us, I feel like I should speak up: condemn you, instead of ignoring the texts on my email and questions passed down from person A to F.

Except you've made sure, one way or the other, that it's both our faults. How we built each other in the start until we had to break apart the taller pieces before one of us became too good for the other.

How we tried keeping each other equals, until we couldn't, and you grew while I perished. In a way, you lost some of the bulk as well, I suppose. I just didn't have anything else left to lose.

Perhaps it's easier this way; having nothing to lose is powerful. Way more powerful than I thought, like how importance, unfortunately, does have a scale.

I still won't completely abandon you though. I can't make myself do that to anyone. Something that isn't the best, but still a part of me I'm proud of.

It's funny: how in ways I'm adopting things from you, some small things I don't notice much. But now, as I have all the time to think, I can see, see how I'm withdrawing and making excuses—thought-out explanations that are a pathway to deceiving like you did.

And it scares me, makes me want to wrap these binds tighter around myself, except they don't go any further, and I'm witnessing myself collapse, not in the best of ways.

Morphing into a variation of you, and me, and everything in between, and it scares me. It terrifies me how I'm almost not bothered at all, not in the ways I'm proud of.

In the end, I guess I still have time to mold myself back into the aspirations I hold for myself. Still build myself up enough to not spill out the right at the wrong times.

There's no conclusion though, something I desperately need in order to close this chapter—no moral or meaning behind anything. Something I strive to accomplish in the small time we are assigned.

Try to leave meaning behind everything and nothing. So when I do go, it's not in vain.

Missing You

I like to think that emotions are just as much a wonder of the mind as our thoughts are; the notion of the heart seems odd when the analogy doesn't fit. Want and need. Not heart and mind.

And the ability of our thoughts to contradict themselves in favor of something negative is quite brilliant, despite the frustration.

There's a place, deep inside where this room lives, for no other reason than to start this loop of incomprehensible love and hate.

It echoes around, hitting walls and barren objects, thudding louder each time.

It's empty, save for those scattered objects; the mess remains there and delivers this collective coherence. They make sense.

I've named the room after you, and I'm not proud of it, ashamed of its existence because even I would rather shut the door and lock it up so it doesn't ever resurface.

But I want to remember; I need to remember you. Because you've left it just so, your imprints still snaking around my back and coming to my chest in an infinite hug.

Your presence always there, the reasons on display, reflecting back in the mirror to show me.

It shows me your sorrow, not your hate, no matter how hard I try searching for it. The way in the end, despite anything, I'd still be there to help you.

How'd you manage that? How'd you manage to make me miss you when I want nothing to do with you? Because such capabilities shouldn't exist to the extent they do.

Yet I miss you. You hear that? I miss you. I miss you so much. And I don't want to; you don't deserve the tides it brings out, because as always, they still only affect me and never you.

Maybe in the end I want to miss you, and need to miss you, mourn who you used to be and who you became. Maybe avoiding it all makes it worse, but it's tiring. And if you won't disappear, I might as well forgive. But I'm not ready yet. Maybe one day. Just not yet.

The thought of letting go only manages to triple the desire to cling onto your presence. Not that it can go anywhere; we're bound by an infinite hug that rots my soul and feeds yours still.

A Piece of You for Me

Your soul will wage war, the tiny piece that's reserved for me. If strong enough, it will make sure of it. It'll try with all its might, until it falls apart from you. Until you lose that piece to me forever.

The day we met was a mistake. I told you then, I tell you now, and I'll tell you the day I leave. The day we met was a mistake. This glitch. This sin.

If we were to stay, then my taint wouldn't have scared you enough to seek my grave in distant lands where your soul wanders at night. And if we were meant to be, then those who are dead would have remained still and silent in my head.

I'll cherish it. I'll forever keep it. Take it with me through the veil, and to a new beginning. I'll wait for it to bloom into you. And I'll walk down a gravelly road and sing a forbidden song. I'll keep you for me. I'll let you flourish.

Time is ticking, and I ask you again and again: do you really want to stay? Stay long enough for the play to end? I don't think you see what

I see when I speak of such things. Because you think this is now, and then will be then. But don't you see I'm stubborn? And harsh? And frustrating?

And slightly, unwillingly indifferent. Numb. Ignorant.

You say you'll pull me over, and I can only hope along this slope, you make the Now separate from the inevitable When. I don't want the When. You have to know I don't want the When. I want the silence. Just the silence.

I'll keep that ghost and wait for the rest of you, maybe even regret. Maybe go to sleep until then, when you come to collect the pieces you lost through people you didn't deserve. If you want, I'll wake, and maybe somehow it will be better then. Maybe the colors and sounds and magic beyond, will corrode the taint.

PART THREE

SUBMERGED

For Anyone Who Needs This

At the end, it's not the overwhelming feelings that throw you over the edge, it's this insurmountable numbness that escalates in a subdued panic.

This murky water that won't let you move, or feel, or talk—and the empty feeling it brings, making you thrash against invisible walls that seem to be dragging you in.

It's this overwhelming need to feel anything, anything at all, to remember anything but this blank slate you're confronted with, and that's when it sounds like a sensible idea to just let go.

What's the point if you can't even feel the need, right?

Except it's not in any way sensible. What of the others reliant on you? Maybe they'll make you feel, even if just remorse for them.

At least it brings back this onslaught of emotions, which, granted, sounds like way too much to deal with, but it's better than subdued panic and empty slates, better than murky water and invisible walls.

So in the end, when you feel nothing, and this invisible closes in on you, know that I'm here, and I promise to be there for you. Know that in this irrevocably corrupt world, I'm here, and my dms are open, and I will do everything to walk you back to the stability of emotions.

And then we can deal with the onslaught together. We'll pick it apart slowly, one by one, until only the wanted emotions reside within us, and we'll be okay.

I'm here for you, and no matter what, even if I don't know, I'll be there to the best of my ability.

INCOHERENT

Melancholy in all its nostalgic victory, tinged with a plethora of fear, tests, and trepidation.

Blurry, but coherent enough to nag and disrupt everything normal.

There's a part of me I don't like putting out. A part of me I fear myself.

This stoic, resolute being, brimming with anger and endurance.

But to those who know, it seems like that being isn't far off, just a few paces away from taking over.

And maybe it won't be the anger that'll tear me to pieces when the time comes. Maybe it'll be the utter hopelessness of all I should have, but couldn't, do.

Of all that seems obvious but isn't: the hopelessness of what could have happened, and what actually did.

Maybe this me that I'm so afraid of is resurfacing, and I've tried for far too long to keep it in.

Spent far too much time letting it stunt me.

But would the difference be detrimental not to me, but to those who know? Would it affect their perceptions and tear at this image of me that they hold?

And if so, does that matter to me? Does it scare me more than letting go?

Deserved Dissociation

In the distance where you stand, mulling over things you wish would just die down, you seem to see yourself come back to life.

It's hard to stay in this groggy haze, yet you manage to control yourself from afar.

It's not that bad, and it is.

Letting reality die down while you're still far away elsewhere, and then there are the times you wish you could try getting full control to speak, to tell them what's actually happening. But it's not like they ever listen, not when it happened, and not now as they come to their own conclusions.

This new reverie of actions that seem damnable.

You let it be because this dissociative silence is better than taking charge and embodying yourself.

It's better to watch in disdain as everything unfolds, rather than becoming yourself and taking charge again.

Slowly Slipping

Just thinking of the twisting, turning roads that lay ahead becomes this canister of unresolved, suffocating thoughts that seem necessarily unwanted.

Maybe it's been too long since foresight sought out the expanse that may turn today around, but energy seems to have evaporated. Diminished.

This sense of wanting that kept thoughts in a reverie of what can happen—vanished.

The care, gone.

And does it not make you ask, So what? So what if it can get better; who cares?

Maybe it's better to change routes, just drift away to high mountains and cold fog. We can still dance from a distance; maybe it'll even bring joy that way, behind this veil where we're just responses. Because it's so much more sincere this way—maybe it's just slipping—except not the way that leaves dread and confusion; a loss, but not the one you thought, just one with less hurt and more comfort.

A slow let-down that won't be so scarring.

Mother Nature's Justification

"A remembrance of what happened, is happening, and will happen."

Amidst this dying land, it seems rather inevitable: this futile attempt at grappling and climbing our way up is rather docile.

Mother Nature's supreme way of levelling this polluted plain.

Rather beautiful. And terrifying.

But fair.

Fair.

Human nature insists that we ourselves are the only living beings that are allowed the chance to fight and maintain our overly obnoxious species.

While this may be true for some, it's rather off-putting to others.

And so, as our numbers decrease and devastation keeps piling on top of us, I can't help but think it's for the right reasons, even when it's probably not.

Tantalizing Ignorance

It's the severity of the words you slip between jolly sentences, hoping, yearning for someone, anyone, to see past the thick congealed coat of hypocrisy you muster.

The ups and downs in your calculated and measured tone that make you want to be vague and obvious. Because you're ashamed, but you still yearn for this small bout of reassurance you think these people can provide.

But sometimes you feel like it's useless, like the obvious staring everyone in the face isn't worth it, because the only thing you can do to keep up with yourself is ignore the tantalizing ignorance and help them with your experience instead.

It's easier that way; they expect you to know and not ask the how, but it's still refreshing.

Because this doled out pain makes helping easier, because others' experiences just seem flawless and easy. And it makes you hopeful, and naive, but utterly happy in this bittersweet pounding in your other-wise dull heart.

And that's okay, because you've come to terms with the ignorance towards you, and it's something you're used to.

And that's okay too, because it's easier, this familiar territory you know how to tread past.

To Those Who Will Get It

The thing is, it'll be way too late when realization's cruel chords strike comprehension. And it will be late, if only because I've laid things out in a camouflage of alright and okay.

Won't be the first time a morbid conscience builds up a revenge unlike others, because unlike the tendencies I'm capable of now, I refrain from hurting myself.

I do want to burn. Yes, but that will come; circumstance won't need to take a chance this time. This time the cards will have already been plagiarized. Already settled corrupted, sticky fingers and selfish intentions I once wanted to get rid of.

I've played my parts. I've honored the act.

And I will continue, except I'll let you direct like you always have. With no resistance. I'll let you handle the strings and continue the show for a little longer. It won't only be you, I assure you.

It'll be all of us that helps me with this, all of us who defeat ourselves.

We'll blow the world, even if not in the literal sense. We'll blow our own little world.

And while it might be my fault entirely, you won't know. Because there's more to directing than the scenes. You'll forget the important things that don't matter until they are fatal. In the end, it won't and will be me.

But most of all, it'll be all of you. All of you who satisfy me.

I won't last because of you, but me, and it'll be blissful. No confrontation. Just guilt, like I feel for no reason. Guilt for no reason and every reason.

I hope you follow soon; we're all damned anyway. But know, no matter how much you might seek me, you might have to live with what you did.

FADING

It was all well and good, if not better, while we were still strangers. Just barely touching and barely keeping up with each other in ways that now embarrass me. We've come too far, and if we fall apart to strangers again, know it wasn't you, but me. Because I won't last long, and it's not in my hands when I actually do leave.

So I'll slowly help us drift so it's not painful at all, just inevitable. And it'll hurt me more than you can imagine. It'll tear at me more than I've ever fathomed, but I won't let it slip this time.

Not for you, but for me.

In My Absence

There are some things that don't seem right. And perhaps most of the time, it's the things we love most that feel this way. They seem far away, yet too close, and it makes you wonder what your presence is to them.

You've had your fair share of slips; you're cracking and chipping away, and you can feel it. You know you're not going to stay long. Not because you don't want to, no, but because you're becoming a detriment. However slowly, you know you're molding into someone else.

And it's far beyond your control now. You can't afford any more slips, can't afford any more spills that echo around until someone adapts. It's the only way, however slowly you follow through, but what seems most frightening is the sheer reality of how leaving will make you hopeless.

And guilty.

No one will see that, not until something happens. And you can't mask yourself anymore, however well-played they were before, without being inauthentic.

It won't be in your hand, for what you want to scream out the most can't come out. Not today, not tomorrow, not until it has to be said by another in your absence.

SELF-REFLECTION

We often forget the intensity of the words we put out there; it's rather disappointing how inconsiderately we might put someone's art to shame with no remorse.

Or how we can openly address our hate for teachers, artists, and parents, and many more equally trying figures out there, without a morsel of regret or disappointment.

How we refrain from learning a whole concept before exaggerating it, and how we forget the depth of all we can perceive, for it's harder to accept, or too inconvenient for our own beliefs.

How it's easy to catch on the wrong words and dismiss all of another person's integrity only because being vultures seems fun, no?

If only we could consider a bit more than just what matters to us. If only we could dig out a bit more empathy and honesty from within us.

It's not a matter of "if" either, I suppose. I'm still learning my flaws, still reflecting on actions, and still realizing things for myself and about others.

How we all have this word limit, and most of them consist of selfish queries and forced ignorance to our convenience.

How we all have an expiration date, yet the severity of these words hasn't clicked yet.

How life's so much shorter than I have previously fathomed, and I might have been the worst in it so far.

How Much?

If only the futility of human nature was more apparent and coherent, for the foes we make, we create, and the realization of such is not enough even to keep us from tearing each other apart.

How small and big perception can be. If only it was tuned in to capture the right things at the right times rather than justifying the right things at all the wrong times. How brittle one's image can get.

So utterly hopeless that our own belief can become at all times the strength you need from them.

So utterly useless at the wrong times, and so much more important when you don't need it.

Maybe if you could scrape the excess of all this strength and need and store it in jars when you need it. But then again, the raw nature from it wouldn't remain sufficient.

In the end, it all just screams meaninglessness no matter how much worth it might seem to hold. In the end, it doesn't matter if you can't derive any need from something.

So tell me, how much need do I possess?

How much of me is needed until I'm no longer meaningful? And tell me, am I just as utterly meaningless as everything else?

What If?

What if you accidentally fell asleep? And woke up, not here, but somewhere else? Not somewhere else, but somewhere entirely different?

What if you snap out of a reality you previously thought was all there was in this world, and you find out you've been living your past again and again?

What if the past, present, and future were all so muddled up, you couldn't tell where you were?

This constant state of urgency kept you up and about? And you could feel previous demons clawing themselves out ... and you knew it was solely your fault? For yes, you might not have caused harm, but this deliberate, undeliberate cycle still has you reliving everything. And that's on you.

What if, what if, it became much worse; you wouldn't just see, you'd hear; you wouldn't just hear, you'd smell, and all your senses were incapable of discerning what really is—because all you know is that something's wrong. But what's wrong and what's right?

What if nothing felt real anymore and you needed someone to remind you again and again what is?

What if you push everyone out because you felt like a black hole tearing everyone and everything apart?

What if it all felt so uselessly chaotic, it was slowly turning you, and all you could think was, *How much longer can I last?*

And then, and then—unexpectedly, out of nowhere—completely spontaneously, you woke up again? And shit—what?

DRIFTING

Through it is the only way.

Distant yet crisp in its embodiment—this loud silence, and not real reality.

Like lucid dreams merging outside the realms of sleep—ironic how trying to escape those only made them come at me faster.

It's weird in a cruel sense. I'd try escaping it all by becoming incapable, intoxicating myself until I couldn't tell what was and what is.

Now, now I'd never do any of it, never willingly.

Give anything to not be lucid or dreaming at all times, even when I'm seemingly awake.

When all I can see is smoke, all I can hear is knocks, and all I can feel is unwanted hands.

I'd do anything to wake up, in all awareness again, and never do anything to compromise it again.

VESSELS

Vessels. Like all that exists, and doesn't.

This capacity, do you feel it? Like this shallow or deep canister, filling and filling.

And all that goes in never comes out. You might scratch and tear at it, trying somehow to pull it open and let some of the entering grains out.

Because maybe you're too full, and your insides feel as though they'll burst, but it won't because you're an endless pit until the day you're gone, bound to live with all that comes in, and all that you give. The tiny ones that belong to you, they keep coming out, from your mouth, and your movements, and your existence, and out of your eyes and nose and ears and mind and heart, and they fill the vessels around you.

Do you think about who your tiny grains will stay within? Never to come to you again. Do you feel this suffocation of having your grains live in those who aren't yours anymore, or are, but not yours to stay with?

Does it not bother anyone else, all these things we've done and will do, just for these grains to fill someone, to fill yourself, to fill nothing up?

But you'll have to stay because even when bits and holes on this vessel open up—through ceaseless, persistent, desperate scratching and scratching—even then nothing pours out? Not even a little.

Because it's endless until we're gone. Nothing and everything and so much and so little. To everyone, and yourself, and no one, and ...

Do you wish your essence would stop marring existence's game, and would just close up and hide inside somewhere not even you can see?

Mend the hole in this bottomless sack that every other existence is bound to be doomed, blessed, bestowed with?

Restless

It lives in my chest, where the rhythm periodically falters; it spins my blood into beautiful red ribbons that supply my mind with poison of the infinite.

My limbs drenched in a thick syrup of fear coating my being. It makes me tingly, all my moves bound by the horror of messing it all up.

Maybe I am restless,
irrational,
maybe I have been made into this.

In An Ideal World

I think, I think I'm just too tired to even hold on anymore, no matter how much I'm deceiving myself.

I think, I think I'd rather stop instead of waiting for something on the other side.

And all those who came and went touched the destitution that his very being represented. All those who came and went were left overcome by the absence and sheer silence of his being.

For as day by day he disappeared, he left more than just a presence; he left an outcome.

An outcome to represent all that could have been, had life been sincere and soft like it's portrayed to be.

PART FOUR

FREEDOM

To Choose Life

Not as tall as the other buildings around, but quite adequate regardless. The air isnt very still, and the cold bellow of air doesn't feel cold at all.

It's not cold at all.

Still quite early, and the sun isn't up yet, but it's quite peaceful up here. Down below, there's a steady trickle of tiny cars, only a few, all running past this building, and I'd like to think I'm in one of them instead of in here.

Think I'll wait until the sun is up. And see what my mind's battling then. But then again, that's probably why I should head back.

Because I'm keeping myself busy getting things done for someone I promised not to do what I'm thinking of doing.

And maybe I should go back. Maybe I should. I should. I should.

But I'm fucking tired, okay? I'm really fucking tired.

And this is probably why I'm already on the stairs, and each foot down is still a hassle, because what the hell, it's right there. There would be no going back after. It'd end. It'd end.

Yet I'm going down, and each floor I cross, the more tired I feel, maybe more with myself than the things I'm running away from. Maybe I'm not so far gone, and maybe I am.

I'm back in the room, and maybe that's for the best. Maybe next time I'll ask to be safe purposefully; maybe they'll tie me down. And I'll ask them to make the straps tighter, tight enough to lock down this crooked thinking.

Lock away the excessive revolution of the same damned memories and the same thoughts. Maybe they'd shut down the parts that have started mimicking all I don't want, again. The words I'm still trying to believe aren't true.

That they'd stop repeating on a loop, where all I can think is, *I'm sorry*. Because I am. If only everyone would listen. I fucking am sorry. So sorry. And so angry. At everything. At myself. At everyone.

I don't like this anger mixing with the tiredness. Because I don't think it'll be good. I don't think I'll be able to keep it at bay.

The Best Parts of the Day

The night's glow feels eerie, and despite it all, it's calming. The illuminating moon's careful existence spreads across the sky in a tantalizing show of freedom.

You can only stare out the small window in your room. The welts on your back are all but a numbing fire now, as you text back to the animated talk of your brother on video.

A small smile plays on your lips as he talks about everything and anything, only texting a response or miming something coherent enough once in a while.

Because for once you're okay with him making all the noise; it's refreshing in a way. You're not expected to do anything, and it feels good. Fresh.

And slowly as your eyes droop and you can perceive the relieved shake of your brother's head, you smile, slipping into a peaceful slumber. The best parts of your day.

This Brother or the Other

It was the small moments, small sparks that emitted from a dormant, years-old bond.

'There's not much I can do.'

And he'd look up. "Keep your shoulders straight and head low. You can do that." He'd say it compulsively. And ironically, it was obvious it was just an annoyed shrug at a lost plea.

And so the sparks would diminish just as fast, and I'd retreat back to a primary house far from where I'm from.

And I'd turn to another equivalent of his. And ask in a statement once again.

'There's not much I can do. Just keep my shoulders straight and head low,' I would text.

And he'd look up just like the other. Except he'd smile and sit next to me. He'd shrug his head. "Whichever dolt said that can go to hell." At my incredulous look, he'd continue, "Keep your shoulders slouched and head held high."

And I'd be left to wonder. Wonder and reminisce whether he'd be the same as the one back home if he'd been there that orange night so long ago?

Sincerity

I have not forgiven; I want to.
I have not been sincere; I have wanted really badly to be.
I don't want to be forgiven; I'm okay with the realistic ending, however hard it is.
I did love; I just wish I hadn't.
I do care about what everyone does; I just don't know how to tell anyone.
I do want to try to get close; I just know he doesn't.
I don't want to be nice unconditionally; I want to be nice about how I convey the negative feelings.

I'm only scared of upsetting because I thought some of you were all I had, or have, or will ever have. Because I don't think I like to impose on others. I am not the best, and that's unfair.

I've muddled up what I want to achieve by blurring the hard parts that it would require. And I want to restart, except I can't erase. I want to be better, more honest, reliable, but I don't know how because it's not expected of me anymore, and so it's harder to convey.

Fleeting Pleasures

There's a marvel in looking down from the top, at the miniscule grains walking around, and the reflective strings of lights that swirl and swirl around when the sun isn't up.

The headlights of traffic merging into hues of red and yellow and orange. The noise dulled by roaring winds, the whole aspect so immensely scary that it calls for you.

It calls for you to fall, and you have to be ready to gather your thoughts, see the tiny squares on buildings and beautiful broken homes; you have to be ready to salvage your will.

Because it's too stunning to not fall over for. Too stunning to not feel the roaring winds and fall and fall until you fly.

Although it seems exhilarating to fall off, I could never back down from where I was made. I was made after fire, and I want to go with it as well.

Seems fitting and deserved; maybe it burns away all the sins I've committed, and lets me forgive myself for all the people I let down.

Just fleeting pleasures, the thoughts of going, not that it'll be soon. I have things I have to do before, promises I need to keep.

Reasons I have to keep me anchored, loved ones I couldn't put through things. And maybe one day I'll find reason in myself, to keep on going. And maybe I'll give reason to others in themselves to keep going.

Maybe I want to leave so bad that it makes me want to stay, if only to give more to someone for themselves.

I have things I have to complete, and although the deviation makes way for more frustration, and more numbness, I suppose it's a step.

Maybe leaving for me will be natural, on its own, my own systems one day collapsing. Maybe that's sooner than I think, or maybe it stretches on for longer.

And the uncertainty of it scares me, because I've found things to do; I can't leave before fulfilling them. And maybe it's made me so that I'm disappointed.

As much as I want to be the one choosing, my uncertainty has become enough for me to make sure, with or without the choice, that hopefully I don't go unfulfilled.

TREADMILL

A distant terrestrial crisis called for a renewed strength to leave behind all that was, to embrace all that is, while focusing on all that will be.

Only a treadmill stood in the way, and it bound you to a cycle of remembrance.

You no longer walked the same streets as you had previously walked with him, and you no longer resided in the familiar room, with your clothes scattered, worn not by you, but him.

But the treadmill has no stop button, and the front remains blank, and the past becomes more vibrant, and colorful, and loud, and fast, and slow.

You no longer visit the same fruitless people again and again, nor do you have to sit hours on end with familiar, yet haunted faces of what was.

You no longer have to be anything, for anyone. And you're free, but you're not. Not when you yourself keep running and running, wearing down the black path of this loop.

And the button should be right there, in the front. And you should be able to see the red digits as time keeps going on and on and on and on.

But you can't. And it's like you're stuck, but where? And why? You know all this, then why? Why? Why?

And it's tiring you out. You're breathing funny, and loudly, and gasping, and your limbs ache, and your mind screams. But you can't stop. You can't.

Because you have to find that stop button, like everyone's telling you to find, but you're too occupied with everything else happening that it makes it blurred and nonexistent.

And no one else can press it for you, but you're tiring out. Quickly. And too slowly.

But it's okay; it's just you; you'll figure it out, maybe sometime later, because your mind's on pause for a while, and you'd rather rest up to gain some energy for the running when it turns back on again.

And that's fine; maybe not okay yet, but fine.

2021

For whatever this is worth, I don't think your coming is any different than having to wake up on any other day in any other year. It's just a normal day, with normal routines, and normal everyday quarrels.

But since your coming holds significance enough to have the whole world celebrate this turning, one way or another, I'll set out to make a single goal for the sake of new beginnings.

This year, I will try my best to stay on top, on top of everything that holds significance, and on top of all that barrels in this year, because no year is a perfect year; they all have their ups and their downs.

And maybe just doing that might make a bigger change than the last year; maybe staying on top before everything buries all motivation will be a change I need to adapt to faster than anything.

So yeah, not that a label can do much with a letter, but here.

With no expectations,
J.

Rain

There's a cohesive story that rain tells, and I'd like to think it's from the dead.

The steady stream that seems so little but is so, so loud, its existence bitter as it comes down from way above to show it's still around.

Sometimes I'd like to think it's a warning of sorts, this angry rant, the loud collisions it makes.

In a pursuit to warn all men there's not much left, not much left, not much left. And we should wake up before we're rain just like them.

A furious bellow towards the sinful and the firm, and calm towards those setting out to be great, as if those who are great and sinful were predefined already.

As if we're made either bad, or good, or both.

I think it whispers its longing toward a world so many want to leave, and it weeps and wails for that ghastly finding, urging, trying to implant the very magnificence earth has to offer in its anguish.

Only to cloud the sky hiding away the light behind their bold, yet subtle existence.

Or maybe it's the bone-weary tiredness of all those who seem so lost and confused. No way forward, no way backward, and no past appealing enough for the light to shine through.

Maybe it's all warnings, pain, and the utter need to awaken something, anything, someday, just once.

And I think it's a guarantee of existence melting into a breeze, into thick or threadlike clouds stretching and showing off this elevated, free existence far above and carefree.

I think it's something I'd like to be: rain. A more cohesive and coherent story with a rhythm both bold and melodious, and so very present.

WHISPERS

They gather, and they talk.
The whispers—I hear them. I hear them.

And I drown in them. I drown in them.
They speak of things, of things I forbid my conscience from forming into one coherent string of words. Those words kill me. They kill me.

And I'd plead for them to stop, but I'm hidden, disguised.
I'm not who I say I am. I'm a fraud. A fraud.

Stuck. Wrapped around whispers, whispers that kill and drown. The water is hot. Boiling.

They don't stop. They don't stop.

As if forgetting is a sin, and they hate me. They remind me. They keep me in place.

But I'm free. I'm free.

The air's not from before, and the dark is way outside.

Outside, concealed. Artificial light bulbs that disappear, that drown, the electricity screeching to stay alive.

But they whisper. They whisper too loudly.

They drown. And the water's hot. Boiling. And fast. And frequent.

Flying away and ignoring them. I want to fly away and ignore them. Wouldn't you? Wouldn't you?

But they always gather too near, and I always feel too lost. Because I'm a fraud. I'm a fraud.

And you can feel it because they look like me when they talk of me. They morph into me, the same eyes, and hair, the same ears, and the same nose. And they look at me, and I'm not them as much as they're me.

And I run. Trust me, I run. Fast. Faster than it's in me to run. But they follow. They always follow.

And they grab onto my ankles and hold onto my shoulders. They pull my hair and scratch my arms. They pull at my neck, and they try to bury me down below.

And they whisper. They come too close. And they whisper.

And I hear them. I hear them.
And I drown in them. I die in them.

Every time. Every goddamn time.

And I would stop them. I know how to stop them.

But they're too many, and they don't care. They keep coming, and they keep whispering.

Each holds a banner of accusations. I deserve them. But I want to get over them. I want to get over them.

And I try. I promise I try.
But they're different. They're all different. But they're still alike. And they drive me crazy.

I'm already crazy. But they drive me crazy. And they won't stop. They won't stop.

They whisper. And pin me down. And come too close. Too close. And they hold banners that yell at them.

The silence yells at me.

My mind yells at me. It wants me gone. I don't want to go. Don't make me go. Don't let me go. Don't let me go.

Today I Turned to Dust

You reached out today; you reached out and crushed the brittle edges I have left, to dust.

You poured the remains from atop a precipice and watched as I flew into nothing with the air.

I roam around everywhere now, scattered through our memories as I miss the way you destroyed me, as I miss the way you broke me and then left me in the hands of an unknown universe.

Today you decided whose love was greater, and you wove a scheme and sent me into woke darkness for days.

Today, I became *yours,* just not in the way you deluded me into thinking.

Today, you shattered me into tiny pieces I'm tired of fitting to be whole again.

And as your existence now remains outside my reach, I can't even cry about it with you by my side.

YOUR GOLDEN STRING

You wove a small, little bird, and he flew to heights unknown, calibrated by the golden string that guided him.

You held that string so tightly, it scorched him as he tried to break away, and the knowledge of such actions intoxicated you.

They freed you, as you tugged and tugged to keep the bird with you. To keep the bird *yours*.

When all the feathers lay blackened on the concrete, the flight stomped out beneath your feet, you let the string go.

And then you let yourself leave.

Only for the flightless, featherless bird to live without the guide it was so accustomed to.

DUST

We're all dusty, covered in a sheen of grey dots so insignificant the tiny grains seem transparent to us. Some people like to dust it off immediately, while others keep it on, ignorant of its existence, and the layers collect until they're hurried inside.

Such was a young girl, covered with layers and layers of dust, and another who was all shiny, and aware, and a bit too clean for the others' liking, and then me, in the middle.

Tell me of a friendship that was consistent throughout, and I'll tell you no such thing exists. Because is it anything if it hasn't tumbled and rolled over a grainy path to meet together at the end?

Maybe both were in the wrong, maybe too much or too little of anything is rather worrying. Maybe that's why I was left behind.

To Be Known

If anyone has ever known me, in all that I have to perceive and project, it's only him and my fairy.

Anyone can try, and assume a portrait of who I might be, and why I might be, but those two, they've seen my all; they'd know all to come and be revealed.

It took quite some contemplation to decide this, to let him have the power of having known me throughout. The worst and best of me.

My inside and outside, my skin and bones, and the hollow behind my eyes waiting for you to fill with what you'd like.

You see, if people are made of dirt, of clay, mine hasn't hardened. It's soft and tearing apart, and someone always needs to mold it into what they'd like again and again so it doesn't melt.

While we were supposed to be each other's, it seemed that eventually only I was his and he was no one's. He still knew me though, and maybe he tried to keep our love sacred, but he couldn't.

I could see he tried. Tried to give back to me what he promised.

PIECE OF HEAVEN

Heaven tore its insides apart to grant me my hidden desires yesterday: a small piece of itself.

It came in the form of the demise of one who called himself mine, to alleviate my heart of his burdens.

Yet now, in practice, it's only faltering; its rhythm is barely there to supply me with the periodic rush of blood everyone seems to need.

If I were to pinpoint my indifference, I would say it was never there for him. I still missed him. Still somewhere, loved him. Maybe still do now.

Redemption

Submerged in a dark sludge,
with no means to find my way,
'til you came and helped me rise out to see

a sky so bleak,
a world so cold,
a goal so vile,
it made me hope.

I hope to show
this perfect feat,
that grabbed me whole
and helped me seek.

A redemption,
some comprehension,
a gentle spark,
to send me scattered.

It rattled doors,
and broke windows,
scarred my hands,
like you meant it to be.

Now you're gone,
and I'm here stranded,
flying off to home in peace.

Reckless Hope

The rusted metal winding about this chest isn't strong enough anymore.

It crumbles about the structure and releases the tight hold to let you breathe.

But do you know what's much more damaging than the release? It's that you're scared to breathe.

The scorched marks will move in and out with each feeling of freedom that slowly enters, clearing the doubt.

And you're not ready to be released.

Because you're still scared to breathe.

Dear nobody, I see an ingenious design.
And it's flawed.

Flickers of Hope

To my Merry.

Merry, you've made the last couple of months one of the best I've ever had. You've been one of the people I've depended on to show me why I've made it as far as I have.

Thank you for being a source of happiness. I couldn't have come out of who I was made, into who I really was, without you.

I may not have always reached out to you, but you were always there for me. Even if I didn't tell you things, even if you didn't know. I just needed to know you were there, and that you could help me out of any bad place I might've been in. And you did. Thank you so much for that.

You're one of three people I hold dearest, that I love most.

I hope you, Roo, and Z stay there for each other. I hope you guys keep each other ok.

I love you so much.

With lots of love,
J (Renley Nicolas Chu)

Dear Roo, Rye, and Merry,

I really hope you all know I love you. You all are pieces of me. And if I were to truly leave, I'd still be living. My Roo is my soul, my Rye is my thoughts and feelings, and my Merry is the spirit in me that makes me giddy.

I love you all so much, I hope you really, really know.

Love,
Kochan/Max/J

Dear Roo, Rye, and Merry,

I've been thinking about how lucky I am lately. How life has still managed to give me one person to have for myself at every stage in life. Jake, even though he has been mean, he was there for me in the beginning, and when he wasn't, it was Elke, and when she left, I had Rye. And now I have my Roo and Merry.

I had my mum and dad in the very beginning, and I suppose there was a time I was left alone. I think I still got to have someone significant for all significant parts of my life.

I suppose God does love me, since despite it all, He didn't leave me completely alone. I had my people. My Roo and my Rye and my Merry. Do you see how all four names are meant to be? Roo, Ren, Rye and Merry.

I love you guys so much.

Love,
Kochan/max/J

B,

I miss how we could think in the same pattern. Miss it a lot. My Roo is very adept at that. She's my everything, you know? You said you wanted me to find someone who could fulfill me before you had to go. I remember. She fulfills me. My Roo makes me who I am. I'm nothing without her.

Recently, she even heard me. I don't like my voice being a constant for someone; you know that. But she heard me, and she said it sounded beautiful.

You would've joined her in making me love it. I was going through screenshots, and I found our conversations for Cryptic. It reminded me of how much we love each other still, of how our love still means something. Sometimes we can hold onto each other from afar. My love is still where it was when you left. At the almost top, except Roo. I love her more. I've found I can love more than I loved you. But I think you'd want me to. It's really nice knowing I can love someone as much as I love my Roo.

I know you'd want me to.

I know I've been scared, but don't worry, I have my Roo. And she'll help me be safe again. I hope you find a Roo too. Everyone needs a Roo.

She knows me completely. I love her so much.

I really hope I can make a Kochan Supremacy (I'm my Roo's Kochan) again. My Roo, you, Merry and Z only. We'll make something big together. Only for us. And we can feel accomplished through it together.

Things are getting better; my Roo is there. I'm forever hers. It makes me very happy—the kinda happy that makes you giddy and excited.

Didn't think I could be like this. I hope she knows how much she is to me. I hope you know how much you are to me.

I'm going home, and I hope whenever you do get this.... Well, I hope you don't, but y'know, that I'm home. I'm so happy. My Roo is the bestest. You would love her. She's like us. She's my everything. I want to live forever for her.

Know I was happy. And I wish I had time to spend with you. I wish I could tell you all about my Roo because it would make you so happy. And I know you need a lot of that too. All of us do.

She made me see so much. I wish I could show it to you. Show you what she's shown me. If I'm gone, I'm gone having seen something beautiful. Someone incredible.

PART FIVE

EVERYTHING

SHIFTING PERCEPTIONS

There's this beauty in human inaccuracy: the way we could try drafting a straight line, but miniature curves, however miniscule, are always present.

This raw warmth of reality, of something so humane and accommodating in ways that make them comfortable.

Typical. Nostalgic.

There's a beauty in being brash, or quiet, calm or not.

A beauty in working, no matter what result lies on the other side.

But the biggest beauty lies in the people who change your life and show you a perspective you had previously hidden behind a pretty curtain of ignorance.

At the Dawning of the World

It all exists.

Sometimes, sometimes it slips, and one forgets, and a sudden disturbance awakens the ripples and the dormant feeling and awareness that it all exists. Like how water moving in a stream is so natural, it doesn't occur to us that the continuous running is, in fact, its stillness, its existence.

There's no turning back, and no taking back, and no forgetting. Because it exists and runs, and that is its stillness—its static state of habit in our memories. Too still it's sometimes completely blended in, tethered to every single thing that exists in the pool of thought and memory and emotion, and whatever else comes with us.

Just like the realization that he himself had gotten away and the other side was empty of anyone else that belonged to him. The others held no capacity to breathe in and out and exist in this big, strong system that no loss yet had rattled away. Of course, back then he was still too young to understand the severity. He knew now though. He did.

Back then he remembered, knowing something was wrong. Felt the loss. Yet he didn't understand what exactly it was that he had lost. And he remembered the loss trickling into every moment to come, waiting for a spark of realization, for a ripple, for a stream to stop moving and restart just to show it was alive.

He grew to know every moment had an absence, an absence that was supposed to either expand an experience of pride, or shrink the existence of pain and grief that one was sure to suffer from living. Because to live is to experience it all, and in all comes the less-than-wanted factors as well.

One can only live so long in their own little normal before it's disrupted with the real norms one sees around them starting to wiggle their way in, destroying that normal. Sometimes, that's not so bad, other times it is. Either way, you have to make do with what is.

The blaze from how it all started, and the flames that have not yet died down, although they seem to be coming to a halt. It seems as though the smoke might never clear out. And so he just clings to the cool existence of something quite impossible. Yet it exists in all its broken, delicate glory and continues to be a companion through everything.

He thinks of those on the other side and thinks of how glad they must be. If they know. If they know, they should be. Because it's the only thing holding him down. Only thing keeping him grounded to the normal, and to the reality of the stream's stillness.

Sometimes a stream needs to stop and run again, to voice its existence. To celebrate its stasis. To celebrate a simple life. To stand at the dawning of a new known world.

ARWEN

Imagine an opening with a lake; all around it are lush trees and rich brown soil, rocks like glitter glistening near the water, and a moonless sky.

Imagine, imagine: fireflies and candles, their collected hues a comforting orange against the navy sky.

Imagine a view as if you're looking at it from a tall mountain peak; everything is too big and gracious and comforting. Everything is calm and collected and burning with so much, so much.

It's exposed and too real, its colors too sharp and belonging, and its knowledge too vast and scary and beautiful.

Think of the whistle made from fast-blowing winds and echoes of their howling through caverns.

Of raindrops falling and fires crackling nearby.

Think of the sound of leaves flapping in the middle of a storm.

Think of crickets, and birds chirping, making an irregular and raw symphony.

Think of all these together and how everything is just the way they seem. Of how sincere it seems.

Words can't possibly describe when you care for someone, it's true.

But we can try, and while human-made words are insufficient, I can always compare to things that have existed way before humankind.

Things magnificent and scarily real.

Arwen, you're an amazing writer and you mean a lot to me.

And however scary that is, I'm glad I have you.

To Be Fully Known and Fully Loved

December 25, 2020

Dear Arwen,

I can't tell the precise moment we became friends in the truest sense. It just happened, I suppose. In the start, we talked, and intentions were not harmful, but neither were they enough to be something that we now have.

Yet we did end up here and even here keeps growing and growing, and it's so much and so vast. I'm glad I know it exists. I'm glad you're here, that while I'm not surrounded by much, somewhere outside of here, you're there, and you're there for me.

This Christmas, more than what the day represents, I'd rather celebrate this friendship we have. I'd rather celebrate how chance gave us to each other, and I'd rather celebrate all that there is to be found through us.

I've always believed life to be a gamble. You play a move and hope it plays right so you don't lose the pieces of yourself you scatter out into the world to be judged and made conclusions about. I gave a piece to you, and you gave me so much more. This time, I really played right. And I'm really glad we're here.

I don't know much. I'm still learning, still exploring, and I value our friendship a lot. I'm no longer scared of the trust I've put in you because you know me; you know all there is, and I love you, and you love me back. And I'm so grateful, knowing that you won't leave, for trusting enough, for trusting you most.

Thank you. Thank you so much, for putting up with me through dumb things, and for staying when you really did not have to. Thank you for having opened a place for me. Thank you for existing. Thank you for making me feel more than this haunted bag no one wants responsibility for.

For Christmas, I wish that one day you will know how much you are as a person, how worth it you are, how much you've impacted me.

For Christmas, I want you to know that I'm trying, and you're one of the biggest reasons why. The biggest reason why one day I will make it. Because I have to. If only for you.

You're a big reason why I'm still here. I'm still here not because you need me, because you don't, and are still here. You've tried telling me how someone's convenience and usefulness don't matter if it comes to true care and love, and you yourself are an example of that.

There's nothing keeping you here. And you know me, know how flawed I am, how imperfect I am. And you're still here.

And I hope both of us get this message you're trying to tell and believe in it stronger one day. Hopefully soon.

I love you. And we may not know how to put it into words. But I do know what's being conveyed. And I'm glad I have you. Haven't been this close to anyone, and as terrifying as the vulnerability is, it's a bit safe. Very safe.

I'm very thankful for that, immensely grateful to have you in my life. You mean so much to me. I hope I never let you down, never disappoint, no matter how inevitable it seems.

I hope I live up to who I should be one day. And I hope that person doesn't disappoint you. I hope you can be proud of that person.

With lots of love,
Justin

Partial Darkness

I held her breath.

If someone was to ask how, months after I should have ceased, I still continued, or why, after having suppressed my existence for that very moment, I was still here; I'd have no choice but to visualize a string connected to mine, stronger than all the other, now broken ones, held together only by her and me in this tug of war holding each other alive.

I'd say, "I have to. I prolonged it. Now I have to." Because I didn't hold my own life, and letting go wasn't on me, but her.

And she was resilient, and somewhere along the lines, I found it made me resilient, only to leave her tired again. Maybe more tired than before.

Partial darkness.

It was still dark, but I could see hues of a distant match held by her, making it easier to bear. And all that was left was to find a worthier reason to hold our string stronger on her end.

My breaths were short and raspy, slow but seemingly dying. And though this didn't seem to promise an end, day by day it seemed as though they'd leave. Moments making me wheeze to try and catch up to them.

I feared having to leave before my time, not for me, but for her.

The breath of someone I held dearest to me.

If they'd ask us why
Why?
Why?
We'd say we hold each other dearer than we hold ourselves.

And perhaps that's why we breathe for each other and keep going. One wants to remain, but give more reason, while the other waits, waits to be delivered.

Perhaps I wait for the day when our breaths come back to be our own responsibility, not because I want to leave, but because there are worthier reasons. And I might—might, might—not have a choice to stay. Or I might not be enough to hold her string together one day.

Perhaps I will wait for the day when the reasons stop, so I can leave. So I can leave.

Reason to Live

There's this glimmer of water that shines and makes the darkness of the sea appealing, this reflection made from the sun's rays, creating a spectrum of blues that says so much more than the stereotypical gloom.

Your existence is like a blue, a blue that's been handpicked from all the blues that the human eye can perceive, and it stretches across my skies and seas, and it chases away the rain and all the dark nights and all the haunting thoughts.

It chases away the night's endlessness and makes room for the day.

It gives me reason, and it gives me hope, and it gives me motivation.

And it is very terrifying.

Thank you for this new hue of fear, that's not there to put me down, but to help me up.

Light has never been so far yet near, and although it is just out of reach, I can make out the direction, and I can sketch out a route, and it's only because of you.

Wish there were words—I'm trying even now—but all letters and all words are insufficient when it comes to expressing who you are to me. And I suppose any other expression would reveal just as lacking. But I still want to.

I'm trying very hard, and I'm only doing it for this new lens that you've introduced to my otherwise-crooked sight. Maybe one day I'll be free of all this; maybe I'll get past everything that has happened; it probably will happen. But it's because I have purpose now.

It is true: my existence is no mistake; I have a purpose. I have a home. I have a safe place somewhere in a person a whole ocean away. And though it's still far away, I'm glad.

You're worth so much more than anything that exists in my spectrum, and your existence is the good in my life. You're so much more than anything I've ever known, and I need you to know that.

I love you and I'm glad we met. I'm so scatterbrained, but you're enough and you're worth so much, so much. Your existence holds a strong portion of how synchronized the universe is for me; you're important, and you matter most to me.

My life is nothing without how much I am to you, and you are to me, because everything else is just bumpy lines. I can't smooth them out for the rest, but somehow our line is smooth, unwavering, and bold—and the only thing I look for when I need to come back.

I haven't seen much of life yet, and that's scary, because I've seen some and it's not so appealing for me to want to see more. But I wish to see it, only if your blue is there to chase away the dark, and only if your marvelous existence will be there to light stars that shine so bright, they chase away the clouds.

Endless Sky

It's been a good while; I don't know the exact date, but more than two weeks since I even stepped out of this room. But today, the trouble it's going to cost me aside, I managed to go out.

I remember talking about the sky with you a while back. You were on a walk, and the sky was artificially blue. Very rich.

And I was thinking, I like this grey sky, with its closed guise and hidden nature. The blue, exposed sky scares me. Probably why I'd rather move to cold places, despite hating winters.

I think it's comforting in a scary way, the clouds, and the cold. I think it's safe.

I hope it's safe.

Missing You

Sometimes I want to tell you I miss you. As if we've met before. Or as if you're already gone.

Sometimes I want to say I miss you, as if I won't be able to say it, and I need to.

I miss you.

Butterflies

I have butterflies inside of me; they're hideous menaces that tear at my walls to be set free. They try to come out, but I make sure to keep them hidden inside so they don't hurt those outside.

My fairy says she can handle them, but I'd rather she keep glowing, and not be unnecessarily hurt any more than she has been.

My silver wings are there in the presence of my Rye, and my gold soul will remain tied to my Roo. My hope-coated hands will reach for my Merry, and we'll make it out. We'll make it out.

Melody of Your Heart

When you came in, a redemption to a mistake I never knew I was making, I admit when things got too much, and I knew I wanted to leave—the noise of every nook and cranny of a vast world mingling together in my head alongside already-existing echoes—I couldn't let you go in favor of the silence.

You were always my shell, my safe place, however long it took me to realize, and your presence hums a constant that keeps me grounded. Whether you were given to me, or I to you, I'm still immensely grateful for it.

In times where nothing seems to be real, a deception that blurs into one long chain of things that can't seem to let me go yet, you shine through them with bright lights and the melody of your heart.

Happiness

May 24, 2021

To my Everything,

There's so much to be said, so much I'd like for you to know, of what you mean to me, of how much you've helped me, of what you've given me; we both know I'm incapable of even comprehending it fully myself, yet like always, we try.

I want to craft this letter beautifully, convey a message I wish would stay with you forever, except there is no message, just the immense love I have for you. More than I've had for anyone in life.

My Roo, you've shown me how much better life can get, of how much I've still to see. And while it may not seem it, these last few months have been the most secure and happy I've felt in a while, in forever.

You've helped me find a need to be something. You've shaped me into a more authentic version of myself, one I've found myself more comfortable in.

You've won in a pursuit to help me recognize that whatever it is God has written for me, for us, it'll essentially be for our good.

If God meant this for us, if everything that has led up to where we are now and what direction we're headed, then I feel I would go through it again if only it meant that I will get to be yours and that you will be mine for longer than is intended.

"He will wipe every tear from their eyes. There will be no more death or mourning or crying or pain, for the old order of things has passed away." -Revelation 21:4.

I've been reading this verse a lot these days, as a form of reassurance, and while I'm still not sure whether this onward the road will be smooth, I can tell I'm off to a safer path with you. Because you're safe, and you're mine and I am yours.

And I'm glad I was given this circumstance to know you, to earn this love I've been yearning and looking for since I've been alone. And not just a love that's left off at friends, but one that has bound me to you in a way that makes me certain, you will be mine and I will be yours. My Roo, you are my soul.

I'm still very amazed that we're really headed where we're headed, that I'm really going to be living with you, that I'm going to be one of you just this week. That I'm already accepted and yearned for as we wait for me to move in and settle.

It feels as though every single wish, every single prayer, want, and need I've ever had is being fulfilled in you. And I'm very thankful for it. I'm extremely thankful for it.

I've been listening to my Christmas present song on repeat, even as I write this letter. The more I hear it, the happier I feel, because it reminds me I'll be with you so soon, that I'll be out of here and get to live however I'd like.

I'll be in my room, with my Roo, with my family.

I love you so much, Roo, so much. You've given me everything I wanted; you've been more than anything I'd dreamed of getting, and you're the reason I get up and eat and sleep, in hopes to recover to be with you soon.

You're my everything; you give me meaning, and you tell me what's needed, and despite me being slightly dramatic and look against it, I feel how much it means. I see how much you care. I see how much you love.

And it makes me think, maybe, just maybe I'm not so wicked. I must've done something to end up with someone as caring and as mine, as you.

I hope someday you know how worth it you are, how enough you are, how brilliant and amazing you are. I hope someday the two of us can sit down and look at each other and say with conviction that we'll make it. That we've made it.

I'm happy, Roo. I'm happy and it's all because of you. I'm smiling and it's all because of you. I'm laughing and it's all because of you. You've given me joy to light up my nightmares with, and you've guided my path home to you.

I'm on my way home, Roo, I'm on my way home to you, and I'm happy about it. I'm proud and happy and I've only ever felt this happiness with you. I'm on my way home to safety, to you. I'm on my way home to be yours forever, so you can be mine forever.

I love you, I love you, I love you.
I love you so much.

From your Kochan,
Renley Nicolas Chu.

Acknowledgements

To those who supported and encouraged during the writing and editing of this book: Michael Chu, Endora Pan, Jesse Wen, Erica Wen, Tony Wen, Jennifer Wen, Sarah Tse, Marwa Farooq, Ebaad Saqib. It's thanks to you we ever got here. Ryan Emerson, for your help in getting this book into the hands of the world. Marwa Farooq, for your help in getting this book into the hands of the world. We love you so much. Ebaad Saqib, for your endless support.

ARC readers, for taking the time to read and review the book, thank you: Ivi Hua, Jon Zacc Regala, Endora Pan, Jesse Wen, C. Ashley Paterno, Sam, Dennis Cao, KJ, Brie, Julia. Jeyran Main of Review Tales, Anthony Avina of Author Anthony Avina Blog, Heidi Wong, thank you for your reviews and input.

Donors, for your financial support to make this dream a reality, O'min Kwon, David Pat, Endora Pan, Tony Wen, Petty Yang, Cam Kuey, Amy Wang, Tina Zhang, Justin and Grace Chang, Jerod Dai, Hannah Tan, Shijun Fang, David Yen, Joanne and Joseph Li, Connie Gong, Josephine and David Cheng, Janelle Ang, Beck Chen, Connie and Timothy Lin, Matthew and Mia Hall, Natalie and Nick Hsieh, Nikki Kumura, James Wen, Tiffanie Chao, Shr-Hau Hung, Linda Velarde, Naixin Zhang, Samantha Chu, Oscar Tsai, Ruthie Caparas.

My editor, Jessica Powers, for your feedback and comments, for honoring the original work and words.

Richard Ljoenes, for your gorgeous cover design.

Natalia Junqueira, for typesetting and designing the book interior.

Made in the USA
Las Vegas, NV
26 September 2021